Workbook for

TONAL HARMONY

with an Introduction to
Twentieth-Century Music

Workbook for

TONAL HARMONY

with an Introduction to Twentieth-Century Music

Third Edition

Stefan Kostka

The University of Texas at Austin

Dorothy Payne

The University of Arizona

Consulting Editor in Music
ALLAN W. SCHINDLER
Eastman School of Music

McGraw-Hill, Inc.

New York • St. Louis • San Francisco • Auckland • Bogotá • Caracas

Lisbon • London • Madrid • Mexico City • Milan • Montreal • New Delhi

San Juan • Singapore • Sydney • Tokyo • Toronto

Workbook for Tonal Harmony with an Introduction to
Twentieth-Century Music

7 8 9 0   SEM   SEM   9 0 9 8 7 6

ISBN 0-07-035882-6

This book was set in Baskerville by Music-Book Associates, Inc.
The editors were Cynthia Ward and John M. Morriss;
the production supervisor was Louise Karam.
The cover was designed by Carol A. Couch.
Project supervision was done by The Total Book.
Semline, Inc., was printer and binder.

Contents

PART THREE: DIATONIC SEVENTH CHORDS

PART FOUR: CHROMATICISM 1

PART FIVE: CHROMATICISM 2

PART SIX: LATE ROMANTICISM AND THE TWENTIETH CENTURY

Workbook for

TONAL HARMONY
with an Introduction to
Twentieth-Century Music

Elements of Pitch

EXERCISE 1-1

A. Name the pitches in the blanks provided, using the correct octave register designations.

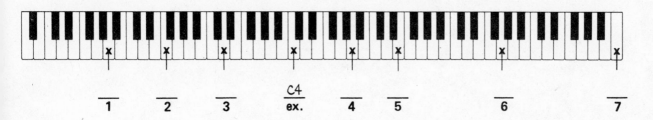

B. Notate the indicated pitches on the staff in the correct octave.

A4   F5   D6   C4   F2   C3   E4   B3   G4   E3   D4   A3

G2   C5   F3   B4   E2   A5   D3   G4   B1   D5   F4   A3   C2   E6

EXERCISE 1-2

A. Notate the specified scales using accidentals, not key signatures. Show the placement of whole and half steps, as in the example.

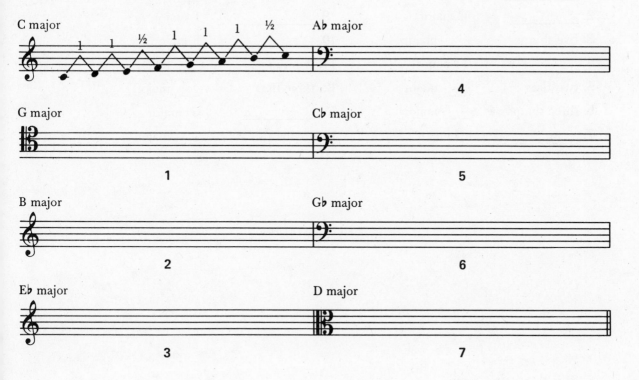

B. Identify these major key signatures.

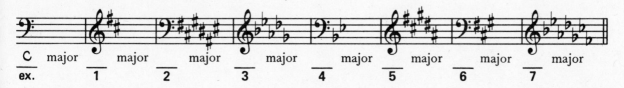

C. Notate the specified key signatures.

3

D. Fill in the blanks.

Key signature	Name of key	Key signature	Name of key
1. _____	D♭ major	8. seven flats	___ major
2. _____	G major	9. _____	F major
3. five sharps	___ major	10. _____	E major
4. _____	E♭ major	11. two sharps	___ major
5. two flats	___ major	12. three flats	___ major
6. three sharps	___ major	13. _____	G♭ major
7. _____	C♯ major	14. six sharps	___ major

4

EXERCISE 1-3

A. Notate the specified scales using accidentals, not key signatures. Circle the notes that differ from the *parallel* major scale. The melodic minor should be written both ascending and descending.

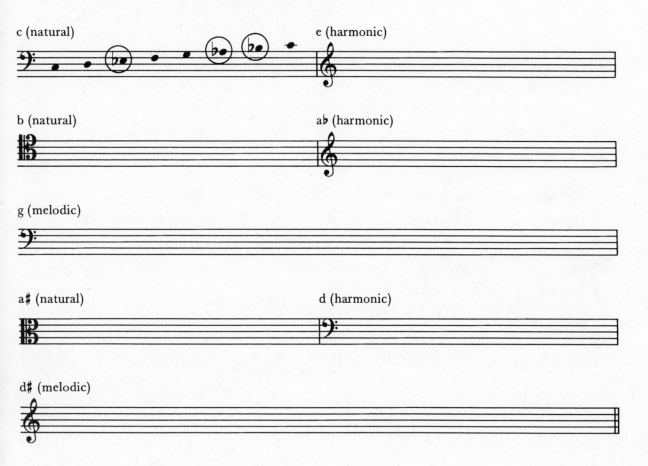

c (natural)   e (harmonic)

b (natural)   ab (harmonic)

g (melodic)

a♯ (natural)   d (harmonic)

d♯ (melodic)

B. Identify these minor key signatures.

a minor   ___ minor   ___ minor   ___ minor   ___ minor   ___ minor   ___ minor   ___ minor
ex.   1   2   3   4   5   6   7

C. Notate the specified minor key signatures.

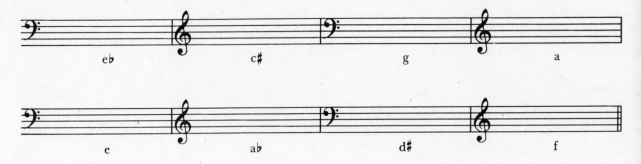

D. Fill in the blanks.

Key signature	Name of key		Key signature	Name of key
1. three sharps	f♯ minor	**8.** _____	g minor
2. _____	e♭ minor	**9.** two sharps	___ minor
3. _____	c♯ minor	**10.** seven flats	___ minor
4. five flats	___ minor	**11.** _____	e minor
5. _____	a minor	**12.** one flat	___ minor
6. four flats	___ minor	**13.** _____	c minor
7. seven sharps	___ minor	**14.** _____	g♯ minor

EXERCISE 1-4

A. Provide the numerical names of the intervals by using the numbers 1 through 8.

B. All of the intervals below are 4ths, 5ths, unisons, or octaves. Put a "P" in the space provided *only* if the interval is a perfect interval.

EXERCISE 1-5

A. All of the intervals below are 4ths, 5ths, unisons, or octaves. Put a "P" in the space provided *only* if the interval is a perfect interval.

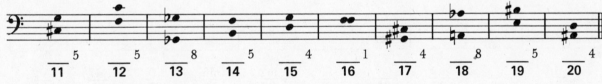

B. All of the intervals below are 2nds, 3rds, 6ths, or 7ths. Put an "M" or an "m" in each space, as appropriate.

$$\underset{21}{}2 \quad \underset{22}{}3 \quad \underset{23}{}2 \quad \underset{24}{}6 \quad \underset{25}{}7 \quad \underset{26}{}2 \quad \underset{27}{}7 \quad \underset{28}{}6 \quad \underset{29}{}3 \quad \underset{30}{}2$$

C. Notate the specified intervals above the given notes.

$$\underset{1}{P4} \quad \underset{2}{m3} \quad \underset{3}{m6} \quad \underset{4}{M2} \quad \underset{5}{P4} \quad \underset{6}{P5} \quad \underset{7}{m2} \quad \underset{8}{P5} \quad \underset{9}{M7} \quad \underset{10}{m7}$$

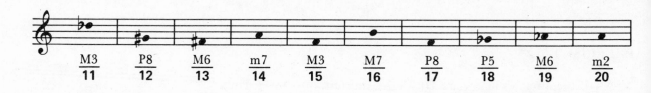

$$\underset{11}{M3} \quad \underset{12}{P8} \quad \underset{13}{M6} \quad \underset{14}{m7} \quad \underset{15}{M3} \quad \underset{16}{M7} \quad \underset{17}{P8} \quad \underset{18}{P5} \quad \underset{19}{M6} \quad \underset{20}{m2}$$

$$\underset{21}{m3} \quad \underset{22}{M2} \quad \underset{23}{M7} \quad \underset{24}{M3} \quad \underset{25}{M6} \quad \underset{26}{m7} \quad \underset{27}{P4} \quad \underset{28}{M7} \quad \underset{29}{M6} \quad \underset{30}{m2}$$

$$\underset{31}{M6} \quad \underset{32}{M3} \quad \underset{33}{m3} \quad \underset{34}{M3} \quad \underset{35}{P5} \quad \underset{36}{m2} \quad \underset{37}{m6} \quad \underset{38}{m7} \quad \underset{39}{M7} \quad \underset{40}{M2}$$

$$\underset{41}{m6} \quad \underset{42}{M2} \quad \underset{43}{P4} \quad \underset{44}{m3} \quad \underset{45}{m7} \quad \underset{46}{P5} \quad \underset{47}{m6} \quad \underset{48}{P5} \quad \underset{49}{M7} \quad \underset{50}{m2}$$

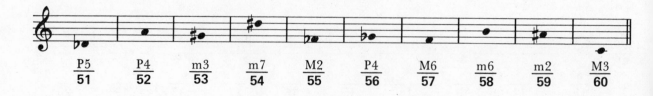

$$\underset{51}{P5} \quad \underset{52}{P4} \quad \underset{53}{m3} \quad \underset{54}{m7} \quad \underset{55}{M2} \quad \underset{56}{P4} \quad \underset{57}{M6} \quad \underset{58}{m6} \quad \underset{59}{m2} \quad \underset{60}{M3}$$

8

EXERCISE 1-6

A. Most of the intervals below are either augmented or diminished. Name each interval.

B. Label what each interval becomes when it is inverted.

1. m3 becomes _____   **5.** M2 becomes _____

2. +5 becomes _____   **6.** +4 becomes _____

3. M6 becomes _____   **7.** P5 becomes _____

4. °7 becomes _____   **8.** m7 becomes _____

C. Notate the specified interval *below* the given note. (You may find it helpful to invert the interval first in some cases.)

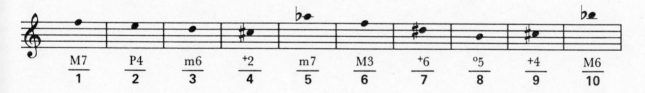

M7	P4	m6	+2	m7	M3	+6	°5	+4	M6
1	2	3	4	5	6	7	8	9	10

m2	M3	+6	M2	°5	m3	°7	P4	+2	+4
11	12	13	14	15	16	17	18	19	20

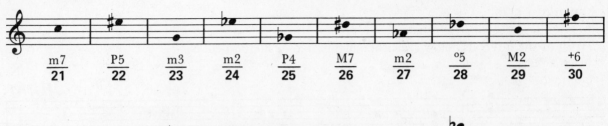

D. Label each interval in this melody (from Wagner's *Götterdämmerung*).

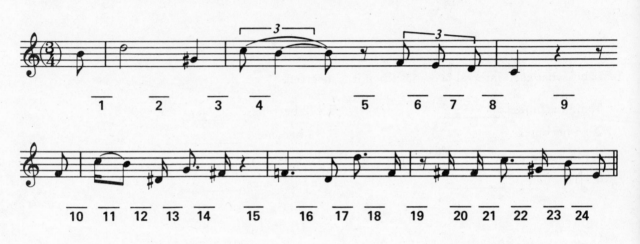

CHAPTER 2

Elements of Rhythm

EXERCISE 2-1

A. Show how many notes or rests of the shorter duration would be required to equal the longer duration.

ex. ♩ x __2__ = 𝅝

1. ♩ x ___ = 𝅗𝅥

2. ♪ x ___ = 𝅗𝅥

3. 𝅘𝅥𝅯 x ___ = ♩ ♪

4. 𝄽• x ___ = 𝄼•

5. 𝄾 x ___ = 𝄼

6. 𝄻 x ___ = 𝄽

7. ♩ x ___ = 𝄻𝄻

8. 𝅘𝅥𝅯 x ___ = ♪•

9. 𝅘𝅥𝅲 x ___ = ♩

10. ♩• x ___ = 𝅗𝅥•

11. 𝅘𝅥𝅯 x ___ = ♩•

12. 𝄾 x ___ = 𝄾

13. 𝄼• x ___ = 𝄻•

14. 𝄾 x ___ = 𝄾•

15. ♪ x ___ = 𝅗𝅥••

16. ♪ x ___ = 𝅝

B. Sing aloud each of the songs listed below. Then identify the meter type of each, using the terms *duple*, *triple*, and *quadruple*.

1. "Auld Lang Syne" _____

2. "Star-Spangled Banner" _____

3. "Pop Goes the Weasel" _____

4. "America" ("My Country, 'Tis of Thee") _____

5. "Swing Low, Sweet Chariot" _____

C. Scale review. Fill in the blanks, using the melodic minor for all minor-key examples.

ex. 6̂ is F♯ in **A** (M)

1. ↓7̂ is C in ___ (m)
2. 4̂ is ___ in c♯
3. ___ is A in F
4. 5̂ is C♯ in ___ (m)
5. 2̂ is ___ in E
6. 7̂ is A in ___ (M)
7. ↓6̂ is ___ in c

8. ___ is C♯ in b
9. 6̂ is C in ___ (M)
10. ___ is F♯ in g
11. 4̂ is G in ___ (M)
12. 5̂ is ___ in G
13. ___ is A♭ in f
14. ↑6̂ is C♯ in ___ (m)

EXERCISE 2-3

A. Fill in the blanks.

	Beat and meter type	Beat note	Division of the beat	Time signature
1.				𝐂
2.	Simple triple	♩		
3.	Simple duple		♫	
4.		♪		2
5.	Simple quadruple		♫	

B. Renotate the excerpts from Example 2-1 using the specified time signatures.

"Jingle Bells"

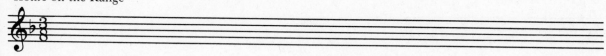

"America the Beautiful"

"Home on the Range"

EXERCISE 2-4

A. Fill in the blanks.

	Beat and meter type	Beat note	Division of the beat	Time signature
1.	Compound triple	♩.		
2.				6/16
3.			♪♪♪	12
4.	Compound duple		♪ ♪ ♪	
5.		♪.		9

B. Renotate the excerpts from Example 2-2 using the specified time signatures.

"Take Me Out to the Ball Game"

"Down in the Valley"

"Pop Goes the Weasel"

14

EXERCISE 2-5

A. Fill in the blanks.

	Beat and meter type	Beat value	Division value	Time signature
1.	Compound quadruple		♪	
2.	Simple triple		𝅘𝅥𝅯	
3.			♩	4
4.		♪.		6
5.				¢
6.			♩	9

B. Each measure below is incomplete. Add one or more rests to complete the measure.

1. $\frac{6}{4}$ 𝅗𝅥. ⌣ 𝅗𝅥. |

2. C 𝅗𝅥.. |

3. $\frac{2}{16}$ 𝅘𝅥𝅱 |

4. $\frac{12}{16}$ 𝅘𝅥𝅮. ♪ |

5. $\frac{3}{8}$ 𝅘𝅥𝅮𝅘𝅥𝅮 ♪ |

6. $\frac{9}{8}$ 𝅘𝅥𝅮𝅘𝅥𝅮𝅘𝅥𝅮 ♩ |

7. ¢ 𝅗𝅥 ⌣ ♪. |

8. $\frac{9}{4}$ 𝅝. |

9. $\frac{3}{2}$ 𝅗𝅥 ♩ ♩ ♩ |

10. $\frac{12}{8}$ 𝅘𝅥𝅮. 𝅘𝅥𝅮. ♩ |

11. $\frac{4}{8}$ 𝅘𝅥𝅮. |

12. $\frac{6}{4}$ ♩ ♩ 𝅘𝅥𝅮𝅘𝅥𝅮𝅘𝅥𝅮𝅘𝅥𝅮 ♩ |

15

C. Provide the best time signature for each measure. In some cases more than one correct answer may be possible.

1. ___ ♪ ♪ ♪ ♫ |
2. ___ ♩ ♫♫♫ |
3. ___ 𝅝. 𝅗𝅥. ♩♩♩ |
4. ___ ♫. ♩ ♫♩ |
5. ___ ♪. ♪. ♫♫ |
6. ___ ♬♬ ♫♩ |

7. ___ ♩ ♫♫♫ ♫♫♫ |
8. ___ 𝅗𝅥. ♩ ♪ ♩ ♫ |
9. ___ 𝅗𝅥 ♩ ♩ ♩ ♫♩ |
10. ___ ♪ ♪ ♪ ♪ ♪. ♪. |
11. ___ 𝅗𝅥. ♬♬♬ |
12. ___ ♪ ♪ ♫ |

D. Each fragment below is notated so that the placement of the beats is obscured in some fashion. Rewrite to clarify the beat placement.

1. $\frac{4}{4}$ ♩ ♫♫♫♫♫♫ | ♪♪𝅗𝅥 𝅗𝅥. | $\frac{4}{4}$ _____

2. $\frac{3}{2}$ 𝅗𝅥 ♩ ♫♫♫♩ | 𝅗𝅥 𝅝 ♩ | $\frac{3}{2}$ _____

3. $\frac{9}{8}$ ♩ ♩ ♩ ♩. | ♩. ♫♫♫♩ | $\frac{9}{8}$ _____

4. $\frac{2}{4}$ ♩ ♬♬♪ | ♪ ♩ ♪ | $\frac{2}{4}$ _____

5. $\frac{12}{16}$ ♪ ♪. ♪♩ ♪ ♪ | ♪.♩ ♫♩ ♪. | $\frac{12}{16}$ _____

6. $\frac{6}{2}$ 𝅗𝅥 ♩ ♩ 𝅝 ♩ ♩ ♩ ♩ | 𝅗𝅥 𝅝. 𝅝 | $\frac{6}{2}$ _____

16

E. Add stems as required.

1. Each duration is a half note.

2. Each duration is a sixteenth note. Beam them in groups of four.

F. Scale review. Fill in the key, scale degree, or note, whichever is missing. Assume the melodic minor form for all minor keys.

G. Interval review. Notate the specified interval above the given note.

H. Interval review. Notate the specified interval below the given note.

CHAPTER 3

Introduction to Triads and Seventh Chords

EXERCISE 3-1

A. Spell the triad, given the root and the type.

1. g _____   **4.** a° _____   **7.** C⁺ _____   **10.** f♯ _____

2. E♭ _____   **5.** f _____   **8.** a♯° _____   **11.** B⁺ _____

3. d° _____   **6.** D♭ _____   **9.** E _____   **12.** e♭ _____

B. Fill in the blanks.

	ex.	1	2	3	4	5	6	7	8	9	10
5th:	G♯	A♭	__	F♯	__	__	__	__	__	B	__
3rd:	E	__	__	__	__	E♭	__	__	B♭	__	A
Root:	C♯	__	D	__	A♭	__	G♯	E♭	__	__	__
Type:	m	M	+	M	m	°	m	M	+	m	°

C. Notate the triad, given the root and the type.

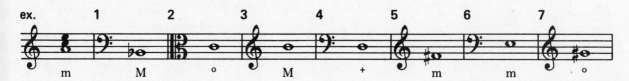

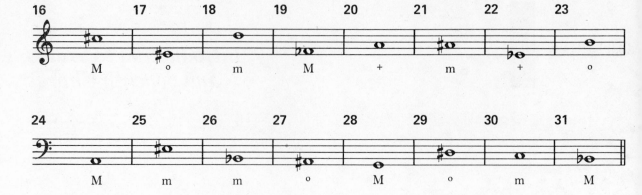

D. Given the chord quality and one member of the triad, notate the remainder
   of the triad.

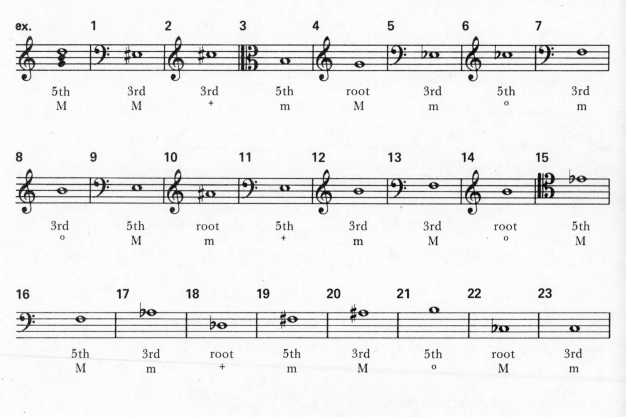

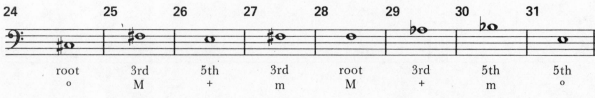

EXERCISE 3-2

A. Identify the type of seventh chord, using the abbreviations given in Example 3-3.

ex. Mm7   1 ___ 2 ___ 3 ___ 4 ___ 5 ___ 6 ___ 7 ___

8 ___ 9 ___ 10 ___ 11 ___ 12 ___ 13 ___ 14 ___ 15 ___

B. Notate the seventh chord, given the root and type.

ex. M7   1 Mm7   2 M7   3 ⌀7   4 Mm7   5 M7   6 °7   7 Mm7

8 ⌀7   9 m7   10 ⌀7   11 m7   12 °7   13 m7   14 Mm7   15 °7

C. Given the seventh-chord quality and one member of the chord, notate the
   rest of the chord.

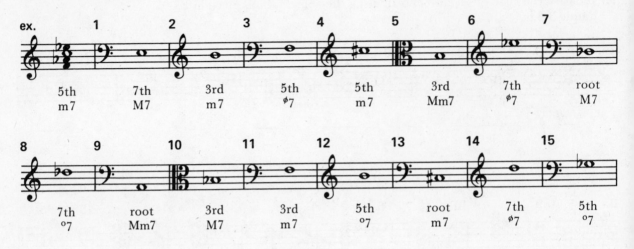

ex.   1   2   3   4   5   6   7

5th   7th   3rd   5th   5th   3rd   7th   root
m7   M7   m7   ⌀7   m7   Mm7   ⌀7   M7

8   9   10   11   12   13   14   15

7th   root   3rd   3rd   5th   root   7th   5th
°7   Mm7   M7   m7   °7   m7   ⌀7   °7

EXERCISE 3-3

A. Identify the root and type of each chord, and show the correct inversion
   symbol.

Root   —   —   —   —   —   —   —   —

Type   —   —   —   —   —   —   —   —

Inversion
symbol   —   —   —   —   —   —   —   —

Root   —   —   —   —   —   —   —   —

Type   —   —   —   —   —   —   —   —

Inversion
symbol   —   —   —   —   —   —   —   —

B. Fill in the blanks below each excerpt with the root and chord type that
   would be played at the corresponding point in the excerpt. The figures
   5 and $\frac{5}{3}$ both mean: use a root position triad.

1. Bach, "Gott lebet noch" (adapted)

2. Bach, "Dich bet' ich an, mein höchster Gott"

   (The first C♯3 in the bass is not to be harmonized.)

3. Corelli, Sonata V, Op. 2, Sarabande

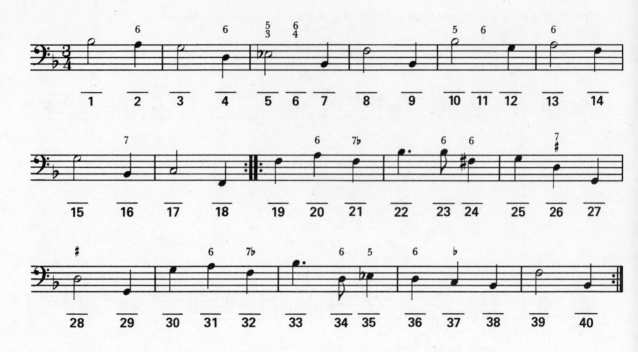

EXERCISE 3-4

A. Identify the root and type of each chord, and show the correct inversion symbol. All the notes in each example belong to the same chord. The lowest note in each example is *the* bass note for the purpose of analysis.

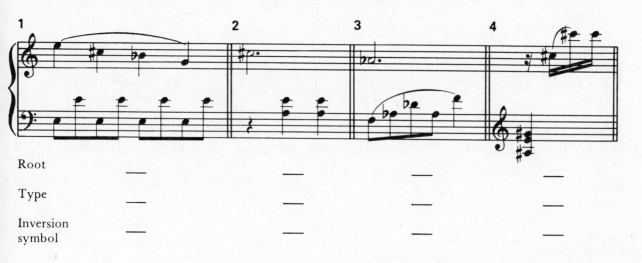

Root   ___   ___   ___   ___

Type   ___   ___   ___   ___

Inversion
symbol   ___   ___   ___   ___

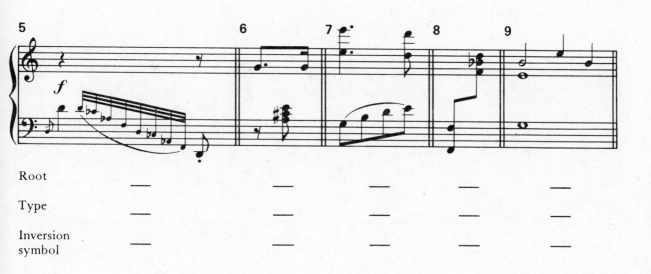

Root   ___   ___   ___   ___   ___

Type   ___   ___   ___   ___   ___

Inversion
symbol   ___   ___   ___   ___   ___

B. The excerpts below are to be analyzed in a similar way. Each chord is numbered. Put your analysis of each chord in the numbered blanks below the excerpt. Notes in parentheses should be ignored for the purposes of this exercise.

1. Bach, "Wer weiss, wie nahe mir mein Ende"

Root _____

Type _____

Inversion
symbol 1 2 3 4 5 6 7 8 9 10 11 12 13 14 15 16 17

Root _____

Type _____

Inversion
symbol 18 19 20 21 22 23 24 25 26 27 28 29 30 31 32 33 34

2. Schumann, "Ich will meine Seele tauchen," Op. 48, No. 5

Root ___ ___ ___ ___

Type ___ ___ ___ ___

Inversion
symbol   **1**   **2**   **3**   **4**

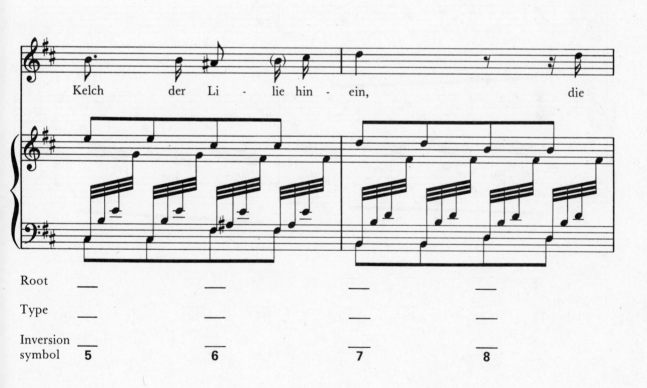

Root ___ ___ ___ ___

Type ___ ___ ___ ___

Inversion
symbol   **5**   **6**   **7**   **8**

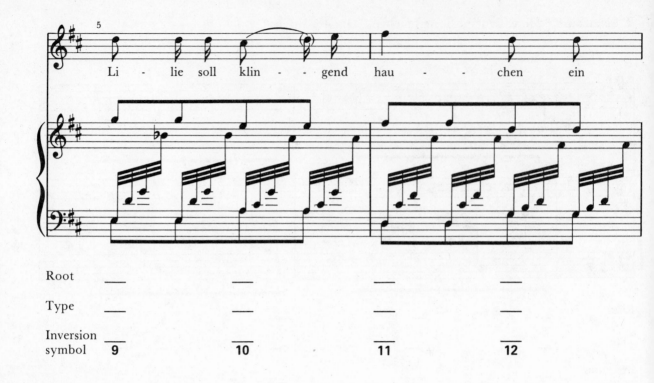

Root   ___   ___   ___   ___

Type   ___   ___   ___   ___

Inversion
symbol   **9**   **10**   **11**   **12**

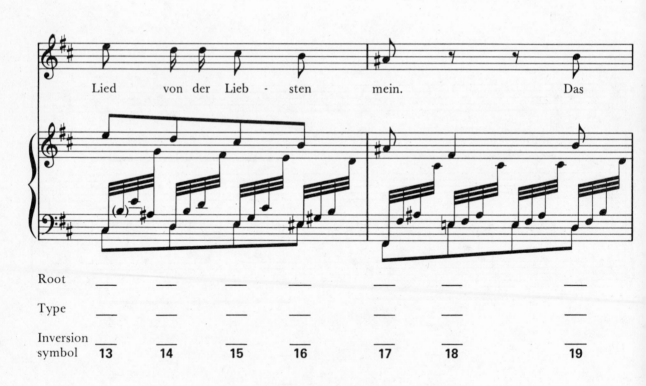

Root   ___   ___   ___   ___   ___   ___   ___

Type   ___   ___   ___   ___   ___   ___   ___

Inversion
symbol   **13**   **14**   **15**   **16**   **17**   **18**   **19**

3. Gottschalk, "Jerusalem"

Root   —

Type   —

Inversion
symbol   1   2   3   4

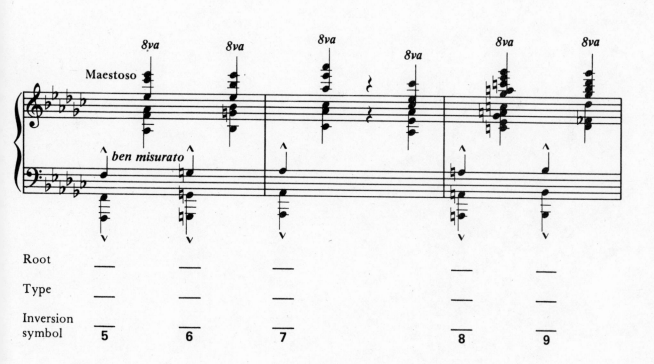

Root   —

Type   —

Inversion
symbol   5   6   7   8   9

CHAPTER 4

Diatonic Chords in Major and Minor Keys

EXERCISE 4-1

A. Given the key and the triad, supply the roman numeral. Be sure your roman numeral is of the correct type (upper case or lower case). Inversion symbols, where required, go to the upper right of the roman numeral (as in I^6).

ex. Ab: vii° 1. Eb: ___ 2. f#: ___ 3. E: ___ 4. g: ___ 5. F: ___ 6. G: ___ 7. c: ___

8. A: ___ 9. c#: ___ 10. Bb: ___ 11. g: ___ 12. Db: ___ 13. c: ___ 14. f#: ___ 15. E: ___

B. In the exercise below you are given the name of a key and a scale degree number (in parentheses). *Without using key signatures,* notate the triad on that scale degree and provide the roman numeral. In minor keys be sure to use the triad types circled in Example 4-7 (p. 65).

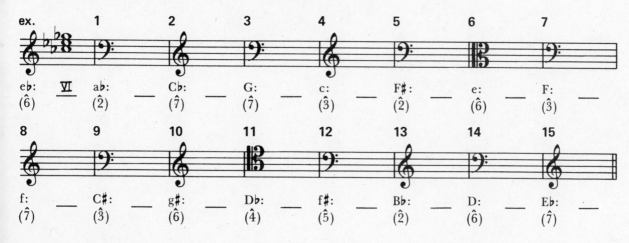

ex. eb: VI (6̂) 1. ab: ___ (2̂) 2. Cb: ___ (7̂) 3. G: ___ (7̂) 4. c: ___ (3̂) 5. F#: ___ (2̂) 6. e: ___ (6̂) 7. F: ___ (3̂)

8. f: ___ (7̂) 9. C#: ___ (3̂) 10. g#: ___ (6̂) 11. Db: ___ (4̂) 12. f#: ___ (5̂) 13. Bb: ___ (2̂) 14. D: ___ (6̂) 15. Eb: ___ (7̂)

C. Analysis. Write roman numerals in the spaces provided, making sure each roman numeral is of the correct type and includes an inversion symbol if necessary.

1. Handel, "Wenn mein Stündlein vorhanden ist"

2. Handel, "Wenn mein Stündlein vorhanden ist"

EXERCISE 4-2

A. Given the key and the seventh chord, provide the roman numeral. Be sure your roman numeral is the correct type and includes an inversion symbol if necessary.

a: vii°⁷ G: ___ c♯: ___ f: ___ B♭: ___ e: ___ A♭: ___ g: ___

d: ___ E: ___ F: ___ A: ___ E♭: ___ b: ___ c: ___ D: ___

B. In the exercises below you are given the name of a key and a scale degree number (in parentheses). Without using key signatures, notate the seventh chord on that scale degree and provide the roman numeral. In minor keys, be sure to use the chord types shown in Example 4-9 (p. 69).

G: iii⁷ B♭: ___ F: ___ b: ___ f♯: ___ A: ___ g: ___ D: ___
(3̂)   (4̂)   (1̂)   (3̂)   (2̂)   (7̂)   (7̂)   (6̂)

c: ___ E: ___ G: ___ E♭: ___ c♯: ___ f: ___ e: ___ A♭: ___
(1̂)   (4̂)   (2̂)   (3̂)   (5̂)   (5̂)   (2̂)   (6̂)

33

C. Analysis. Put roman numerals in the spaces provided, making sure each roman numeral is of the correct type and includes an inversion symbol, if needed.

1. Beethoven, Variations on a Theme by Paisiello

2. Brahms, "Minnelied," Op. 44, No. 1

PART **II**

CHAPTER **5**

Principles of Voice Leading

EXERCISE 5-1

A. Criticize each melody in terms of the rules for simple melodies discussed on pages 78-79.

1

F: I   —   V   I   IV   —   I   IV   I

2

e: i   —   V   i   V   i   V   i   iv   V   i

3

D: I   IV   V   I   V   I   —   IV   I

B. Compose simple melodies that will conform to these progressions.

1

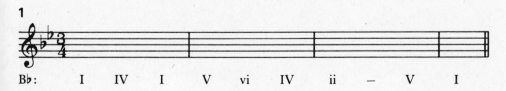

B♭:   I   IV   I   V   vi   IV   ii   —   V   I

2

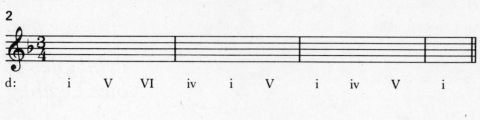

d: i V VI iv i V i iv V i

3

G: I iii IV I V I IV V I

EXERCISE 5-2

A. Analyze the excerpt below, using roman numerals. Then show beneath
   each roman numeral the structure of the chord by writing "C" or "O" for
   close or open structure. The notes in parentheses are not part of the chord
   and should be ignored for the purpose of harmonic analysis.

Schumann, "Roundelay," Op. 68, No. 22

B. Review the two conventions concerning spacing on page 82. Then point
   out in the example below any places where those conventions are not
   followed.

C. Fill in the circled missing inner voice(s) to complete each root position triad, being sure that each note of the triad is represented. Follow the spacing conventions and stay within the range of each vocal part.

d: iv   Eb: ii   b: i   D: V

G: IV   e: V   Bb: iii   g: i

EXERCISE 5-3

A. Label the chords in the excerpt below with roman numerals. Then label any examples of parallelism (objectionable or otherwise) that you can find.

Bach, "Ermuntre dich, mein schwacher Geist"

B. Find and label the following errors in this passage:

1. Parallel 8ves

2. Parallel 5ths

3. Direct 5ths

4. Consecutive 5ths by contrary motion

5. Spacing error (review p. 82)

C. Find and label the following errors in this passage:

  1. Parallel 8ves
  2. Parallel 5ths
  3. Direct 8ves
  4. Spacing error

CHAPTER 6

Root Position Part Writing

EXERCISE 6-1.   **Using repeated triads**

Fill in the inner voice or voices in the second chord of each exercise. The
key is F major throughout.

1 four parts

2 three parts

EXERCISE 6-2.   Using roots a 4th (5th) apart

A. Add alto and tenor parts to each exercise below. Each progression involves
roots a P4 (P5) apart. Use one of the three methods outlined on pages 93-94
in each case, and state which you have used.

c: V   i   G: ii   V   I   V   E♭: iii   vi   ii   V   I

b: i   iv   i   V   i   F: vi   ii   V   I   IV   I   V   I

a: V   i   iv   i   D: iii   vi   ii   V   I   V   I

B. Add an alto part to each exercise. Be careful to observe conventions concerning spacing, parallels, and doubling. Each triad should include at least a root and a 3rd.

F: ii   V   I   IV   I   f#:   i   V   i   iv   A: iii   vi   ii   V   I

EXERCISE 6-3. Using roots a 4th (5th) and 3rd (6th) apart

A. Add alto and tenor parts to each exercise below. Use the smoothest voice leading in each case.

F: I vi IV ii   g: i V i VI iv i   D: I vi ii V I

Eb: I iii vi ii V I   e: i VI iv i V i

B. Add an alto part to each exercise below. Be careful to observe the conventions concerning parallels, spacing, and doubling.

Eb: IV ii V I   b: i III VI iv i   G: I V I IV ii V I

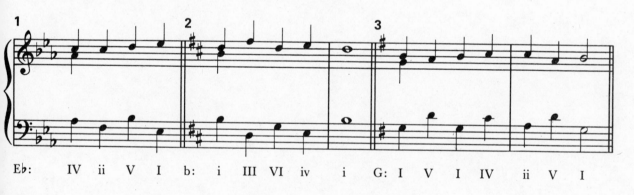

F: I IV ii V I   d: i iv i VI iv i V i

45

EXERCISE 6-4. Using all root relationships

A. Complete each progression. Make two versions of each, one for three parts and one for four parts.

1 three parts   four parts

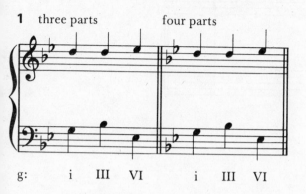

g: i   III   VI   i   III   VI

2

D: ii   V   I   ii   V   I

3

a: iv   V   VI   iv   V   VI

4

B♭:   V   I   vi   V   I   vi

5

G: I   vi   V   I   vi   V

6

F: vi   ii   V   vi   ii   V

B. Fill in alto and tenor parts in these exercises.

1

A: I vi IV V I IV ii V — I

2

f: i V i VII III iv V — i

3

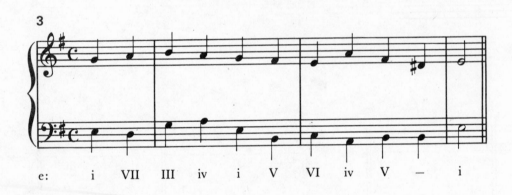

e: i VII III iv i V VI iv V — i

4

B♭: I — — V I V vi IV V I

5

d: i   IV   V   i   III   iv   V   i   VI   iv   V   i
           (not)
            iv

C. Add three upper parts to each figured bass to make a four-part choral texture. Review figured bass symbols (pp. 51-53) if necessary. Try to follow
all of the spacing and voice-leading conventions discussed in this chapter.
Label the chords with roman numerals.

1

2

D. Write the following short progressions in root position for combinations
   of three and four parts.

1 three parts

Eb: ii   V   I   c#:   i   VI   iv   A: IV   V   vi

2 four parts

Eb: ii   V   I   c#:   i   VI   iv   A: IV   V   vi

F: I   iii   IV   D: vi   ii   V   g: VI   iv   V

EXERCISE 6-5

A. Notate the chords below for the specified instruments. Each chord is written at concert pitch, so transpose as needed for the performers. Use the correct clef for each instrument. Note that the instruments are listed in score order, the order used in Appendix A, which is not always the same as order by pitch.

Fl.	Ob.	Clar. in B♭	Bsn.	A. Sax
T. Sax	Hn. in F	Tpt. in B♭	Trb.	Hn. in F
Vla.	Vl.	Vc.	D.B.	Tuba

B. Set the following progression for combinations of three and four parts.
   If possible, score for instruments in your class. Use root position only.

1 three parts (reduced score)

d: i   iv   V   VI   iv   V   i

(full score)

2 four parts (reduced score)

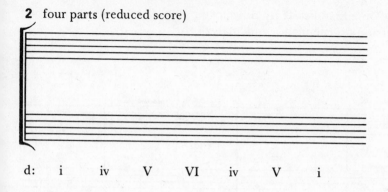

d: i   iv   V   VI   iv   V   i

(full score)

C. Write a version of the excerpt below on a grand staff by transposing the
parts to concert pitch. Play your version on the piano, and analyze the
harmonies if you can.

CHAPTER 7

Harmonic Progression

EXERCISE 7-1

A. Complete each progression to conform with the chord diagrams on pages 117-118. The chord in the blank should be different from those on either side of it. In most cases, there is more than one correct answer.

1. IV ___?___ I (___ or ___)   **4.** iii ___?___ V (___ or ___)

2. vi ___?___ I (___ or ___)   **5.** vii° ___?___ vi (___ or ___)

3. I ___?___ ii (___ or ___)   **6.** vi ___?___ ii (___)

B. Bracket any portions of these progressions that do not conform to the chord diagrams on pages 117-118.

1. i   vii°   i   iv   VI   V   i

2. I   vi   ii   IV   I   V   I

3. I   iii   IV   vii°   I   IV   V   I

4. i   III   iv   i   iv   V   vii°   i

C. Analysis. Label all chords with roman numerals, and bracket any successions of chords that do not agree with the chord diagrams on pages 117-118.

1. Bach, "Du Friedensfürst, Herr Jesu Christ"

2. Vivaldi, Cello Sonata in G Minor, Prelude. Unfigured bass realization by S. Kostka.

Non-chord tones in the solo part have not been put in parentheses, but the harmonic analysis can be done by concentrating upon the accompaniment. The key is g minor, in spite of what appears to be an incorrect key signature. Key signatures had not yet become standardized when this work was composed.

D. Analyze the chords specified by these figured basses, and add inner voices to make a four-part texture. Bracket all circle-of-fifths progressions, even those that contain only two chords.

1

2

3

E. Analyze this figured bass, then add a good soprano line and inner voices.
   Bracket all circle-of-fifths progressions.

F. Add an alto part (only) to mm. 1-2. Then compose a good soprano line
   for mm. 3-4 and fill in an alto part.

F: I   V   I   vi   IV   V   I   vi   ii   V   I   V   I

G. Harmonize the melodies below by using root position major or minor (not diminished) triads in an acceptable progression. Try to give the bass a good contour while avoiding parallel and direct 5ths and 8ves with the melody. Be sure to include analysis. Finally, fill in one or two inner parts, as specified by your instructor.

1

G:

2

D:
or b:

3

E♭:

4

d:

5

E:

H. Compose a *simple* melody, then follow the instructions for Part G. You
   may need to revise the melody as you work on the harmonization.

I. Review: Label the chords with roman numerals and inversion symbols
   (where needed).

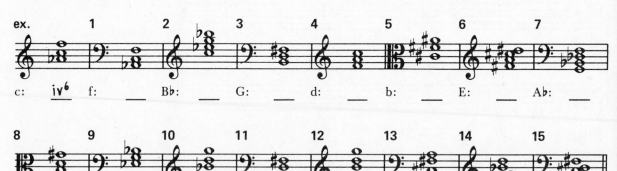

ex.   1   2   3   4   5   6   7

c: iv⁶   f: ___   Bb: ___   G: ___   d: ___   b: ___   E: ___   Ab: ___

8   9   10   11   12   13   14   15

f#: ___   g: ___   Eb: ___   D: ___   e: ___   c#: ___   F: ___   A: ___

CHAPTER 8

Triads in First Inversion

EXERCISE 8-1

A. Analysis.

1. Bracket the longest series of parallel sixth chords you can find in this excerpt. Do not attempt a roman numeral analysis. Does the voice leading in the sixth-chord passage resemble more closely Example 8-8 or Example 8-9 (p. 130)?

Beethoven, Sonata Op. 2, No. 1, III

2. Label all chords with roman numerals. Then classify the doubling in each inverted triad according to the methods shown in Example 8-10 (p. 131).

Bach, "Was frag' ich nach der Welt"

3. Label all chords with roman numerals. Bracket the circle-of-fifths progression (review pp. 109-110).

Handel, Passacaglia

B. The excerpt below is from Mozart's String Quartet K. 428. Supply the missing tenor line (viola in the original).

E♭:   I⁶ $\frac{5}{3}$ 6   IV   I⁶   IV   V$\frac{4}{3}$ I   V⁶ $\frac{5}{3}$

C. Supply alto and tenor lines for the following passages.

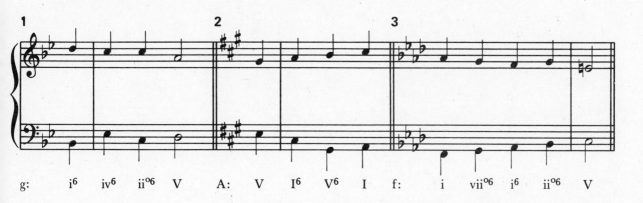

g: i⁶   iv⁶   ii°⁶   V   A: V   I⁶   V⁶   I   f: i   vii°⁶   i⁶   ii°⁶   V

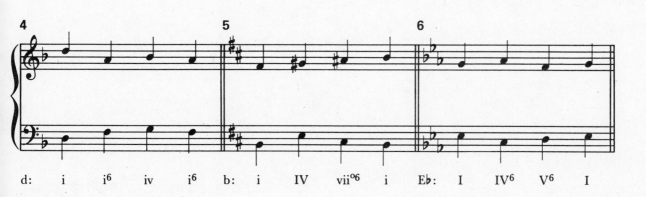

d: i   i⁶   iv   i⁶   b: i   IV   vii°⁶   i   E♭:   I   IV⁶   V⁶   I

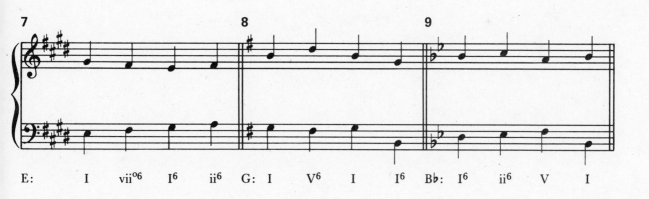

E: I   vii°⁶   I⁶   ii⁶   G: I   V⁶   I   I⁶   B♭:   I⁶   ii⁶   V   I

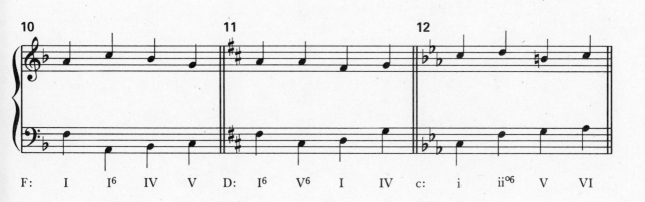

F: I   I⁶   IV   V   D: I⁶   V⁶   I   IV   c: i   ii°⁶   V   VI

D. Supply alto lines for the following passages.

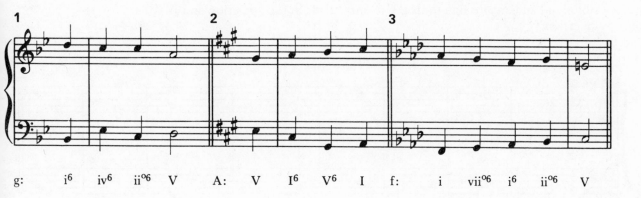

g: i⁶   iv⁶   ii°⁶   V   A: V   I⁶   V⁶   I   f: i   vii°⁶   i⁶   ii°⁶   V

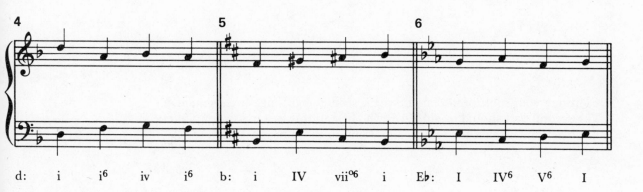

d: i   i⁶   iv   i⁶   b: i   IV   vii°⁶   i   E♭:   I   IV⁶   V⁶   I

E. Analyze the harmonies implied by the soprano/bass lines below, and add one or two inner parts, as specified by your instructor.

F:

e:

F. The following passage is reduced from Beethoven's Sonata Op. 10, No. 3, III. Analyze the implied harmonies (more than one good solution is possible) and add an alto line (only). Use only triads in root position and first inversion.

G. Continue your solution to Part D with a second eight-measure segment. The second part should be similar to the first, but if it starts exactly like it, objectionable parallels will result. Maintain the three-part texture.

H. Review pages 51-53. Then realize the figured basses below by following these steps:

   a. Provide the roman numerals specified by the figured bass.

   b. Compose a simple melody that will conform to the progression and at the same time will avoid objectionable parallels with the bass.

   c. Make two completed versions of each, one for three parts and one for four parts.

1

Bb:

2

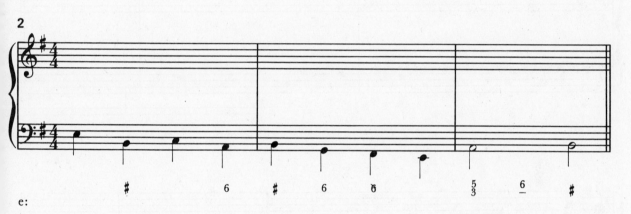

e:

I. Review the chord diagrams on pages 117-118. Then assign roman numerals to each of the bass notes in the exercises below, using triads (only) in root position and first inversion to create a good tonal progression. Then follow steps b and c for Part H. If possible these settings should be for vocal or instrumental combinations found in your class.

J. Select roman numerals with which to harmonize this melody, changing
   chords every place there is a blank. Be sure your progression is a good
   one. Then write out the melody with a bass line, using first inversion
   triads where appropriate. Make sure the bass sounds good when played
   with the melody and that there are no objectionable parallels. Finally,
   make a piano setting, using the bass line you composed. Keep the piano
   texture simple, perhaps like that in Example 8-3 (p. 126).

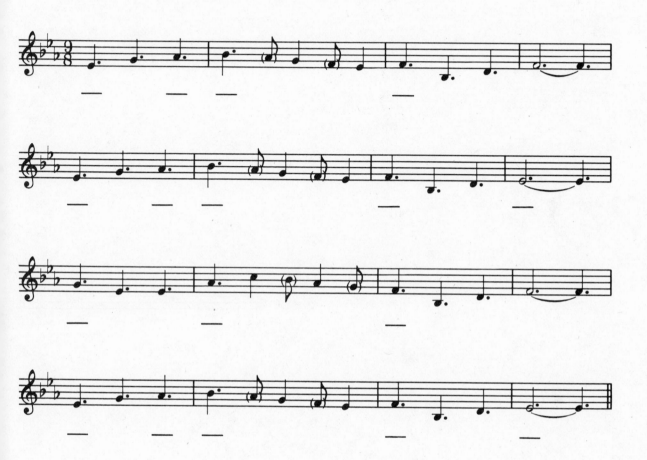

CHAPTER 9

Triads in Second Inversion

EXERCISE 9-1

A. Analysis. In addition to the specific instructions for each example, label each six-four chord by type.

  1. Label all chords with roman numerals.

Schumann, "The Wild Rider," Op. 68, No. 8

  2. Label chords with roman numerals.

Handel, "Wenn mein Stündlein vorhanden ist"

3. Label the chords with roman numerals, and put parentheses around all non-chord tones. The bass in m. 87 is E throughout.

🎧 Beethoven, Sonata Op. 2, No. 3, III

4. In this excerpt, six-four chords are formed by arpeggiations in m. 1 and by a melodic bass in m. 2 (the bass in mm. 2-3 imitates the soprano melody in mm. 1-2). Put roman numerals in the blanks provided, and put parentheses around all non-chord tones. Then show where any six-four chords occur, no matter how briefly.

🎧 Bach, English Suite No. 2, Courante

B. Fill in one or two inner parts, as specified. Identify any six-four chords by type.

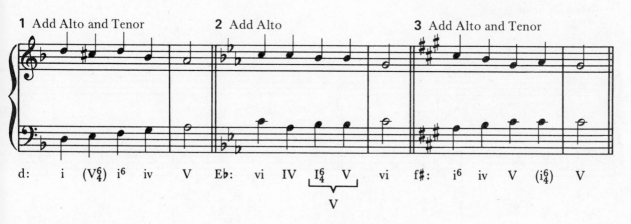

1 Add Alto and Tenor   2 Add Alto   3 Add Alto and Tenor

d: i (V$^6_4$) i^6 iv V   E♭: vi IV I$^6_4$ V vi   f♯: i^6 iv V (i$^6_4$) V

V

4 Add Alto and Tenor   5 Add Alto

B♭: I (IV$^6_4$) I vii^{o6} I^6 IV V   a: i v^6 iv^6 (i$^6_4$) ii^{o6} V i

C. Realize these figured basses for three or four voices, as specified. Notice the frequent use of $\frac{5}{3}$ (or the equivalent, such as $\frac{5}{\#}$) to indicate root-position triads following an inverted chord. Analyze with roman numerals and label six-four types.

1 Add Soprano, Alto, and Tenor   **2** Add Soprano and Alto

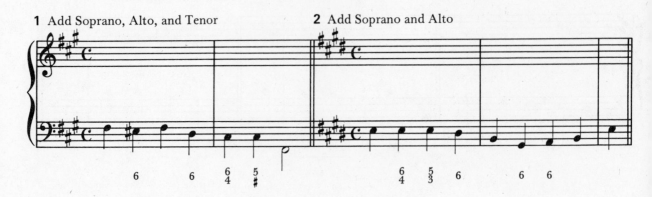

3 Add Soprano, Alto, and Tenor   **4** Add Soprano, Alto, and Tenor

D. Harmonize each unfigured bass with a good tonal progression. Then compose a soprano line that will fit the progression without creating objectionable parallels with the bass. Finally, fill in alto and tenor parts to make a four-part texture. Be sure to include a six-four chord in each one, and identify the six-four type.

E. Continue the accompaniment of this violin melody. Non-chord tones are in parentheses. Be sure to use at least one cadential, passing, or pedal six-four chord. Include a harmonic analysis.

CHAPTER 10

Cadences, Phrases, and Periods

EXERCISE 10-1

A. Cadences. Using only triads in root position and first inversion, make up examples of the following cadences. Each example should include three chords—the two cadence chords plus one chord preceding the cadence chords. Include key signatures and roman numerals.

1 three parts   **2** four parts   **3** three parts   **4** four parts

A: ___ ___ ___   g: ___ ___ ___   F: ___ ___ ___   b: ___ ___ ___
(root position IAC)   (DC—careful!)   (HC)   (inverted IAC)

5 three parts   **6** four parts   **7** three parts   **8** four parts

G: ___ ___ ___   d: ___ ___ ___   Bb: ___ ___ ___   e: ___ ___ ___
(PAC)   (PC)   (leading-tone IAC)   (Phrygian HC)

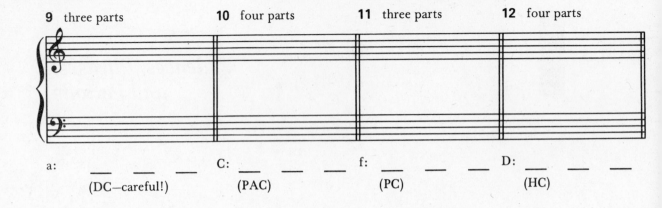

| **9** three parts | **10** four parts | **11** three parts | **12** four parts |

a: ___ ___ ___   C: ___ ___ ___   f: ___ ___ ___   D: ___ ___ ___
   (DC—careful!)   (PAC)   (PC)   (HC)

B. Analysis. The cadence chords have been analyzed for you in each example.

1. Make a diagram of this excerpt similar to the diagrams used in the text.
   Include phrase labels (a, b, and so on), cadence types and measures,
   and the form of the example.

Schumann, Symphony No. 1, Op. 38, III (piano reduction)

2. Diagram the form of this excerpt. Also:
   a. Bracket all sequences in the melody.
   b. Find the best example of imitation between the melody and the bass.
   c. Label the chords implied by the two voices. Non-chord tones are in parentheses in the bass (only). Note: The best choice for m. 5 is *not* a ii chord.

Anonymous: Minuet in G, from the *Notebook for Anna Magdalena Bach*

3. Diagram the form of this excerpt, and copy out any rhythmic motives found in both of the phrases. The progression at *x* resembles an IAC in what key? What is the relationship between that key and e minor?

Mendelssohn, *Song Without Words,* Op. 62, No. 3

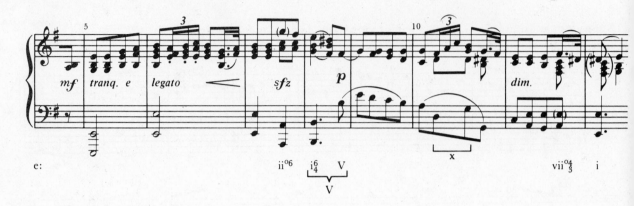

4. This excerpt is in the form of a three-phrase period (some would call it a phrase group). Would it be better to say that it has two antecedent phrases or two consequent phrases? Why? Which phrase features a circle-of-fifths sequence? Analyze all of the chords in that phrase, and diagram the form of the excerpt.

Mozart, Sonata K. 545, I

G:

V^4_2

V^6 I

V^7 I

5. Diagram the form of this excerpt in three ways, all of which are possible interpretations: (1) all four-measure phrases: 4+4+4+4+4; (2) two long phrases plus a short final phrase: 8+8+4; (3) two phrases, the second extended: 8+12. Which interpretation do you prefer? Why?

Mozart, Sonata K. 310, III

6. Diagram the form of this theme, then label the first five chords. Also, see if you can find a disguised sequence hidden in the soprano and another in the bass in mm. 1-8.

Beethoven, Sonata Op. 13, II

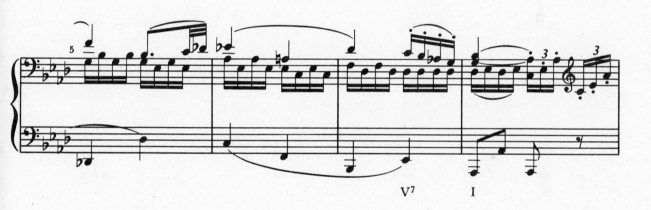

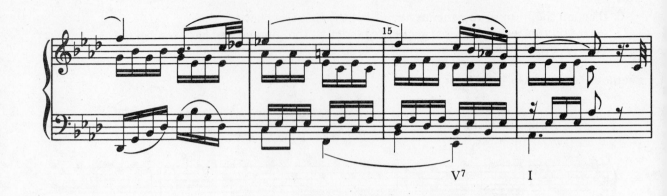

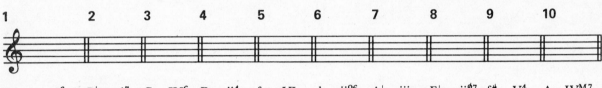

C. Review. Notate the chords in the keys and bass positions indicated.

E: I^6 Bb: vi^7 G: IV^6_4 D: ii^4_3 f: VI d: vii^{o6}_5 Ab: iii Eb: $vii^{ø7}$ f#: V^4_2 A: IV^{M7}

CHAPTER 11

Non-Chord Tones 1

EXERCISE 11-1

A. Analysis.

1. Go back to Example 6-9 (p. 99), which shows NCTs in parentheses, and identify the type of each NCT in the blanks below. Always show the interval classification (7-6, and so on) when you analyze suspensions.

Alto: ____ ____ ____

Tenor: ____ ____ ____ ____

Bass: ____

2. Analyze the chords and NCTs in this excerpt. Then make a reduction similar to those seen in the text by (1) removing all NCTs, (2) using longer note values or ties for repeated notes, and (3) transposing parts by a P8 where necessary to make the lines smoother. Study the simplified texture. Do any voice-leading problems appear to have been covered up by the embellishments? Discuss the reasons for the leap in the tenor in m. 3.

Bach, "Hilf, Herr Jesu, lass gelingen"

reduction

B. After reviewing pages 179-184, decide what *one* suspension would be best
in each excerpt below. Then renotate with the suspension and at least one
other embellishment. Remember to put parentheses around NCTs and to
label NCTs and arpeggiations.

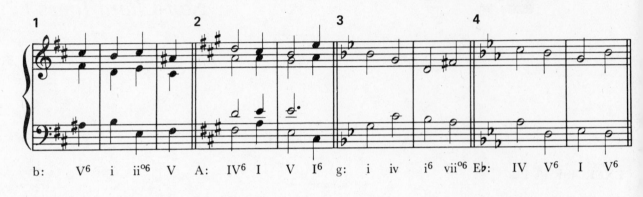

b: V⁶   i   ii°⁶   V   A: IV⁶ I   V I⁶ g: i   iv i⁶ vii°⁶ Eb: IV V⁶ I   V⁶

C. The example below is a simplified excerpt from a Bach chorale harmonization. Label the chords with roman numerals, and activate the texture with
stepwise NCTs. Label all embellishments.

Bb:

D. In the figured basses below, the symbols "4 #" call for a 4-3 suspension, with a sharp applied to the note of resolution. The symbols "6 —" indicate that a first inversion triad is to be used above both C's in the bass.

For each figured bass, do the following:

1. Analyze the harmonies with roman numerals.

2. Fill in one or two inner parts, as specified.

3. Add some stepwise NCTs to each example, and label them.

1

2

E. Using the following progressions, compose a good soprano/bass framework, using inversions where desired. Next add one or two inner parts, as specified. Show with an *x* every possible location for a 9-8, 7-6, 4-3, or 2-3 suspension. Finally, create an elaborated version of the simple texture, including at least one suspension. Other embellishments should be limited to arpeggiations and stepwise NCTs.

1. Three-part texture. (Remember that diminished triads should be used in first inversion.)

e: i | vii° i | iv i | iv i | ii° V | i |
3/4

2. Four-part texture.

A: I   V   vi   ii | V   vi   IV   V | I |

F. Compose your own harmonic progression, and follow the instructions for
   part E. Try a two-, three-, or four-part texture.

G. Analyze the chords implied by this two-voice framework. Then embellish the framework in an arrangement for string quartet. A suggested beginning is given.

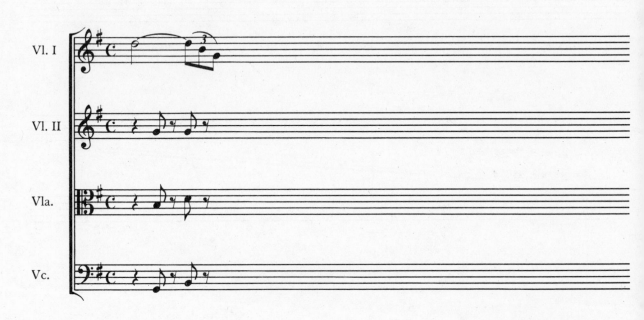

H. Continue your solution to Part G to form a parallel period.

CHAPTER 12

Non-Chord Tones 2

EXERCISE 12-1

A. Analysis.

1. Go back to Example 7-18 on page 117 of the text, where NCTs are
shown in parentheses, and identify the type of each NCT in the blanks
below. Always show the interval classification (7-6, and so on) when
you analyze suspensions.

m. 1 ____ ____   m. 3 ____ ____

2. Do the same for Example 10-14 on page 165 of the text.

m. 10 ____   m. 11 ____   m. 13 ____ ____ ____

m. 14 ____   m. 15 ____   m. 16, violin: ____   piano: ____ ____

3. Do the same for Example 9-13 on page 148.

Vl. I: m. 23 ____   m. 24 ____   m. 25 ____   m. 26 ____

Vl. II: m. 23 ____   m. 26 ____ ____ ____

4. Label chords and NCTs in this excerpt.

Schumann, "Roundelay," Op. 68, No. 22

A:

5. Label chords and NCTs in this excerpt. Then diagram and label the form.

Mozart, *Eine kleine Nachtmusik,* K. 525, II

(IV⁶₄)

6. Label the chords and NCTs, but do not included the pitches called for by the turns (in mm. 1 and 3). Bracket any melodic sequences you find.

Beethoven, Sonata Op. 10, No. 1, II

B. Using a three-part texture, write authentic cadences in five different keys, employing a different NCT from the following list in each cadence: p, n, ant, app, e.

C. Compose a simple melody for each figured bass below, and fill in inner voices to make a four-part texture. Include some of the NCTs studied in this chapter. Analyze chords and NCTs.

1

g:

In this example, use a V chord on beat 3 of m. 1. Also, the symbols "6 — —" mean that a first inversion chord is to be maintained throughout m. 2.

2

F:

D. Compose a passage in four parts in the key of b minor employing a 7-6 suspension near the beginning and a tonic pedal near the end.

E. Compose eight measures to continue Part A, number 6, on page 92 of this Workbook. Maintain a similar texture, and end with a PAC. Include an NCT studied in this chapter.

F. The framework below is a simplified version of a passage from Mozart's
   Magic Flute. Embellish the framework, turning it into a vocal part (to be
   sung on neutral syllables) with piano accompaniment. Try to include at
   least one chromatic NCT.

G. Continue your solution to Part F to form a parallel period.

PART **III**

CHAPTER **13**

The V⁷ Chord

EXERCISE 13-1

A. The note given in each case is the root, 3rd, 5th, or 7th of a V⁷ chord. Notate the chord in root position, and name the major key in which it would be the V⁷.

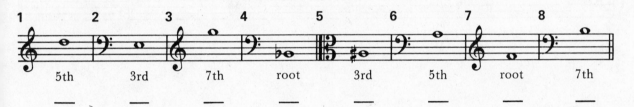

B. Analyze chords and NCTs in the excerpt below. Then discuss the voice leading in the two V⁷ chords. (Note: You may have analyzed the B's in the V chords as passing tones, but consider them to be chord 7ths for the purposes of your discussion.)

Bach, "Wir Christenleut'"

C. Resolve each chord to a root position I. (Note: *c* means complete chord,
   i means incomplete chord.)

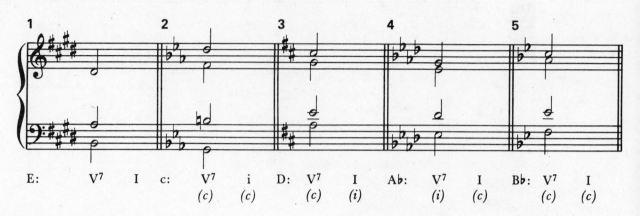

E: V⁷   I   c: V⁷   i   D: V⁷   I   A♭:   V⁷   I   B♭:   V⁷   I

(c) (c)   *(c) (i)*   *(i) (c)*   *(c) (c)*

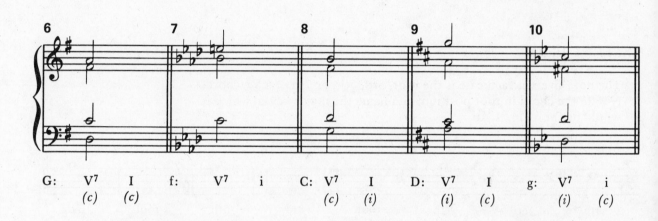

G: V⁷   I   f: V⁷   i   C: V⁷   I   D: V⁷   I   g: V⁷   i

(c) (c)   *(c) (i)*   *(i) (c)*   *(i) (c)*

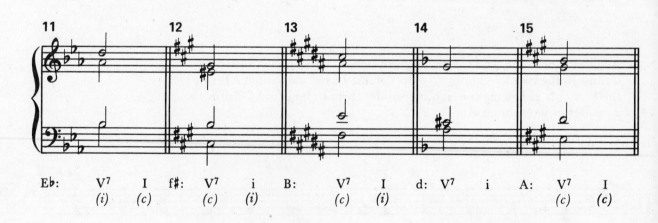

E♭:   V⁷   I   f♯:   V⁷   i   B: V⁷   I   d: V⁷   i   A: V⁷   I

(i) (c)   *(c) (i)*   *(c) (i)*   *(c) (c)*

98

D. Notate the key signature and the V⁷ chord, and then resolve it.

1 three parts   **2** three parts   **3** four parts   **4** four parts   **5** four parts

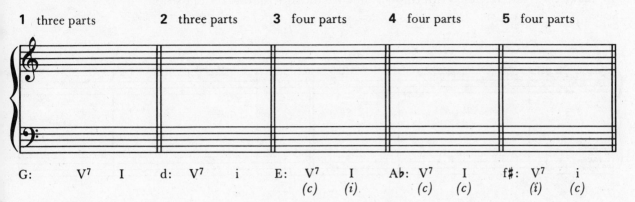

G: V⁷   I   d: V⁷   i   E: V⁷   I   A♭: V⁷   I   f♯: V⁷   i
                                          (c) *(i)*   *(c)* *(c)*   *(i)* *(c)*

6 three parts   **7** three parts   **8** four parts   **9** four parts   **10** four parts

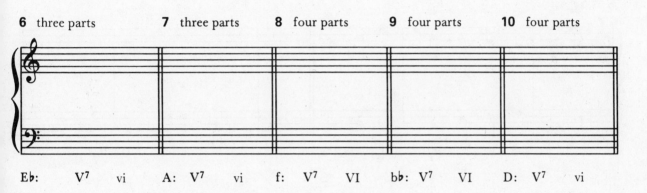

E♭:   V⁷   vi   A: V⁷   vi   f: V⁷   VI   b♭: V⁷   VI   D: V⁷   vi

E. Analyze the harmonies implied by these soprano/bass frameworks. Then
make four-part versions with embellishments and at least one root position
V⁷ chord.

F. Analyze the chords specified by this figured bass. Then make two harmonizations, one for SAB chorus and one for SATB chorus.

1

2

G. Analyze the chords implied by the soprano and bass lines below. Then fill in inner parts. Remember that the tenor part sounds a P8 lower than written.

H. Set a short text for four-part chorus. The text might be a poem, a headline from a newspaper, anything. Include at least one V^7-I progression. Try to keep the motion going through the use of elaborations.

I. Compose a period in a simple three-part texture. End the first phrase with a V^7-vi DC, the second with a V^7-I PAC. Then create a version for three instruments, the top part being elaborated by arpeggiations and NCTs, the other two parts in an accompanying role. Turn in both versions.

1. simple version

2. elaborated version

EXERCISE 13-2

A. Notate the specified chords. Use accidentals instead of key signatures.

Db: V_5^6 a: V_3^4 Eb: V_2^4 D: V_3^4 c: V_2^4 F: V_5^6 b: V_2^4 E: V_5^6

B. Label chords and NCTs in the excerpts below. Comment upon the treatment of the leading tone and 7th in any V^7 chords in root position or inversion.

Notice that in Exercises 1 and 3 the key signature does not agree with the given key. This is because in each case the music has modulated (changed key) to the dominant. Modulation will be introduced in Chapter 18.

1. Bach, "Ich dank' dir, lieber Herre"

(Which is the more sensible analysis of beat 4 of m. 3: iii_4^6 or V^6?)

F:

2. Beethoven, Sonata Op. 2, No. 1, III

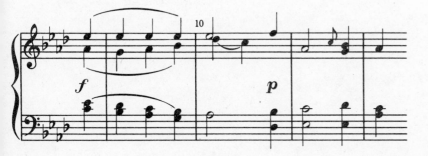

3. Mozart, Quintet K. 452, I (piano reduction)

Bb:

4. Schumann, "Im Westen," Op. 25, No. 23
(Do not label NCTs in this excerpt.)

mich   und mein Kind - lein   an's   Herz____   ged - rückt.

C. Resolve each chord to a tonic triad (except as indicated). Analyze both
   chords.

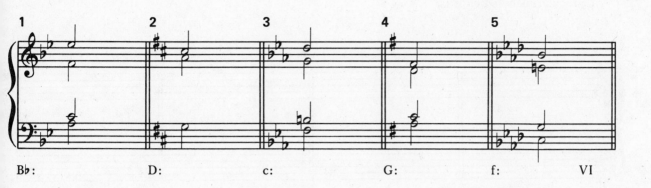

Bb: D: c: G: f: VI

C: f#:   f#:   g: Ab:

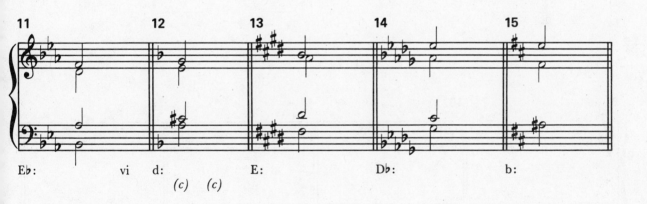

Eb: vi   d: E: Db: b:
                  (c)   (c)

D. Supply the key signature. Then notate and resolve the specified chord.
Finally, begin the passage with a chord that will allow good voice leading
and provide the indicated approach to the 7th. Notate as quarter notes.
Label all unlabeled chords.

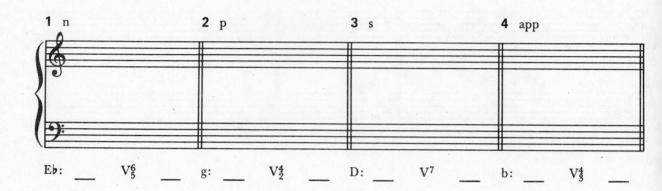

1 n   **2** p   **3** s   **4** app

E♭: ___ V$^6_5$ ___   g: ___ V$^4_2$ ___   D: ___ V^7 ___   b: ___ V$^4_3$ ___

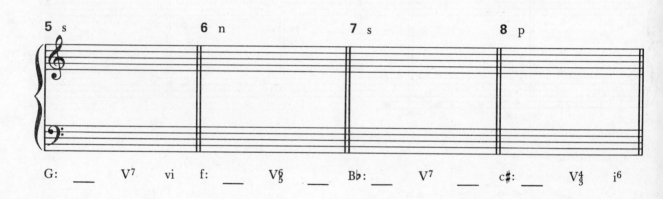

5 s   **6** n   **7** s   **8** p

G: ___ V^7 vi   f: ___ V$^6_5$ ___   B♭: ___ V^7 ___   c♯: ___ V$^4_3$ i^6

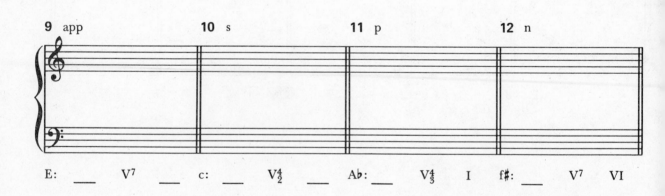

9 app   **10** s   **11** p   **12** n

E: ___ V^7 ___   c: ___ V$^4_2$ ___   A♭: ___ V$^4_3$ I   f♯: ___ V^7 VI

E. Analyze the chords implied by each soprano/bass framework. Then add
inner parts and embellishments to make a four-part choral texture. Include
an inverted V⁷ chord.

1

2

F. Analyze the chords implied by this soprano/bass framework. Then create a piano texture by filling out some of the chords and adding embellishments. Arpeggiations will be especially useful for prolonging the I chord in mm. 1-2. Be sure to include an inverted V^7 chord.

G. Make one or more settings of the following song.

1. Write an arrangement for two B♭ trumpets, unaccompanied. Analyze the harmonies implied by the two lines. Include at least one inverted V^7.

2. Make an arrangement for four-part chorus. Try to elaborate the other voices slightly. Include at least one inverted V^7. Watch out for parallel 8ves and 5ths throughout.

3. Compose a version for piano solo, including at least one inverted V^7. Be prepared to play it, or find someone else in the class who will do so.

H. Compose a period for a string trio (violin, viola, cello) or for some other combination of instruments in your class. Include at least two inverted V^7 chords.

CHAPTER 14

The II⁷ and VII⁷ Chords

EXERCISE 14-1

A. Notate the following chords. Use accidentals, not key signatures.

B. Analyze the following chords. Be sure your symbols indicate chord quality
   and inversion.

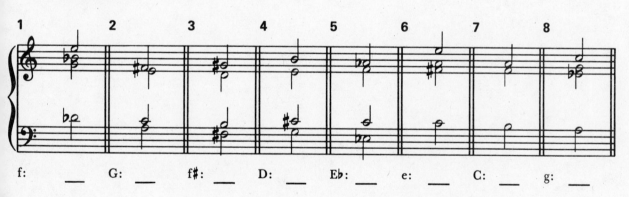

C. Analyze the chords and NCTs in the following excerpts. Whenever a ii^7 (ii$^{\phi7}$) or vii$^{\phi7}$ (vii^{o7}) chord is encountered, discuss the voice leading into and out of the chord.

1. Bach, "Jesu, der du meine Seele"

2. Bach, "Herzliebster Jesu, was hast du verbrochen"

b:

3. Label the chords in the blanks provided. Do not label NCTs in this excerpt. The *m.v.* dynamic markings stand for *mezza voce,* "half voice," which means approximately the same thing as *mezzo forte,* or *mf.* The tempo is *Poco Adagio.*

Haydn, Quartet Op. 50, No. 6, II

4. Do label the NCTs in this excerpt. These are the third and fourth phrases of the five-phrase double period that makes up the opening theme. Although too long to be quoted here, the entire theme (mm. 1-30) is worth studying.

Haydn, Quartet Op. 20, No. 4, I

D. Notate, introduce, and resolve the specified chords. Approach each chord
7th as a suspension, a neighbor, or a passing tone, as specified. Include
key signatures and roman numerals.

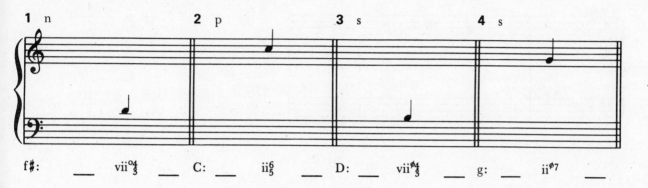

1 n   2 p   3 s   4 s

f♯: ___ vii°$^4_3$ ___   C: ___ ii$^6_5$ ___   D: ___ vii°$^4_3$ ___   g: ___ ii^{ø7} ___

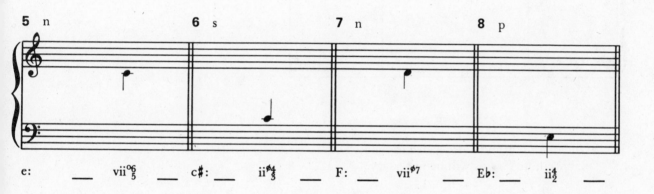

5 n   6 s   7 n   8 p

e: ___ vii°$^6_5$ ___   c♯: ___ ii$^{ø4}_3$ ___   F: ___ vii^{ø7} ___   E♭: ___ ii$^4_2$ ___

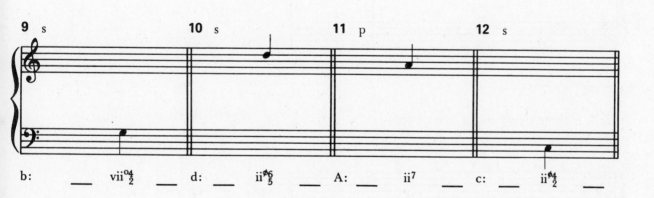

9 s   10 s   11 p   12 s

b: ___ vii°$^4_2$ ___   d: ___ ii$^{ø6}_5$ ___   A: ___ ii^7 ___   c: ___ ii$^{ø4}_2$ ___

E. Harmonize these chorale phrases for four-part chorus.

1. Include a root position ii^7.

G:

2. Include a root position vii^{o7} and a 4-3 suspension.

g:

3. Include a ii$^{\phi 4}_{2}$ and a deceptive cadence. Some eighth-note chords will be necessary.

d:

4. Include a vii$^{\phi 4}_{3}$ and a passing tone.

C:

F. Make a setting of the folk song below for some combination of voices and/or instruments available in your class. Include one of the chords discussed in this chapter.

CHAPTER 15

Other Diatonic Seventh Chords

EXERCISE 15-1

A. Notate the following chords. Use accidentals, not key signatures.

1	2	3	4	5	6	7	8
Ab: I^{M7}	g: $\#vi^{\emptyset7}$	G: vi^6_5	f: III^{M6}_5	b: i^7	Bb: IV^{M4}_3	a: VI^{M7}	e: iv^4_2

9	10	11	12	13	14	15	16
Eb: IV^{M4}_2	c: i^4_3	c#: IV^7	F: vi^7	E: I^{M6}_5	f#: iv^4_3	d: VI^{M6}_5	A: iii^4_2

B. Analyze the following chords. Be sure your symbols indicate chord quality and inversion.

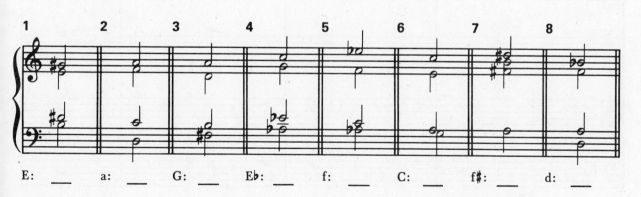

E: ___   a: ___   G: ___   Eb: ___   f: ___   C: ___   f#: ___   d: ___

C. Analyze the chords in the excerpts below. Comment upon the voice leading involving any of the chords discussed in this chapter.

1. Schubert, *Moment Musical,* Op. 94, No. 6

A♭:

1   2   3   4   5

2. Bach, "Herr Jesu Christ, du höchstes Gut"

3. Corelli, Concerto Grosso Op. 6, No. 1, VII

D: iii

4. Haydn, Piano Sonata No. 30, I

After you finish labeling the chords, complete the three-part reduction of mm. 86-92 that follows the excerpt.

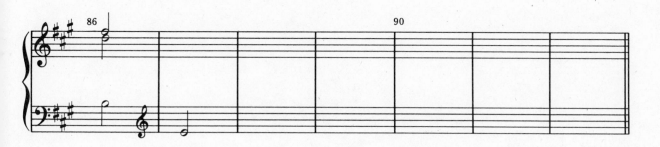

D. Continue this four-part elaboration of Example 15-19 (p. 247). Use B♮ throughout. Do not analyze with roman numerals.

E. Notate, introduce, and resolve the specified chords. Approach each chord 7th as a suspension, a neighbor, or a passing tone, as specified. Include key signatures and roman numerals.

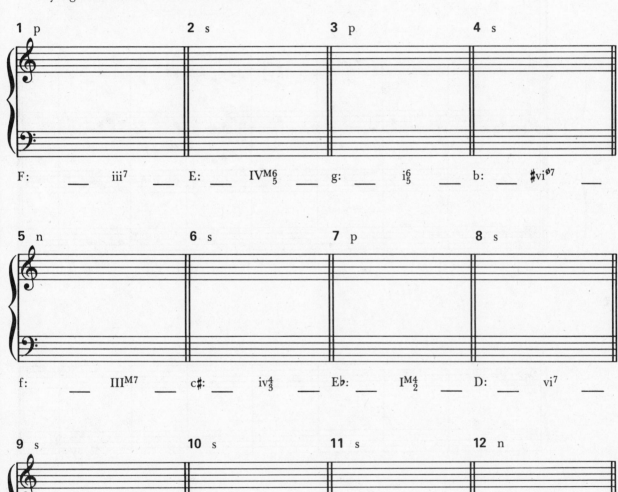

F. Analyze the chords called for by the figured bass below. Then continue the four-part realization of that figured bass. Note: be sure to review pages 246-248 before proceeding. (Figures in the fifth measure added by the authors.)

Corelli, Concerto Grosso Op. 6, No. 12, V

Realization

G. Compose a passage for three voices or instruments containing a sequence
   of seventh chords similar to that used in the excerpt of Part F.

H. The following is a simple note-against-note contrapuntal framework. Analyze the implied harmonies, then elaborate it into a passage containing several seventh chords. Use four parts or a free keyboard texture. Your final version might be complex, but the original framework should be retained. Include roman numerals and NCT analysis.

I. Create a framework similar to that above, but in the minor mode. Be sure
    that it implies a good harmonic progression. Then create an elaboration
    that employs some of the seventh chords discussed in this chapter. If pos-
    sible, score for a combination of instruments in your class.

Secondary Functions 1

EXERCISE 16-1

A. Review the material on spelling secondary dominants (pp. 258-259). Then notate these secondary dominants in the specified inversions. Include key signatures.

<table>
<tr><td>1</td><td>2</td><td>3</td><td>4</td><td>5</td></tr>
<tr>
<td>c#: V^7/iv</td>
<td>Ab: V^6/V</td>
<td>c: V^4_3/VI</td>
<td>e: V^6/III</td>
<td>F: V^4_2/ii</td>
</tr>
</table>

<table>
<tr><td>6</td><td>7</td><td>8</td><td>9</td><td>10</td></tr>
<tr>
<td>D: V^6/vi</td>
<td>b: V^7/V</td>
<td>A: V^6_5/iii</td>
<td>g: V/iv</td>
<td>a: V^4_2/V</td>
</tr>
</table>

<table>
<tr><td>11</td><td>12</td><td>13</td><td>14</td><td>15</td></tr>
<tr>
<td>Eb: V^6_5/IV</td>
<td>f#: V^6/VII</td>
<td>C: V^7/ii</td>
<td>Bb: V^4_2/IV</td>
<td>G: V^4_3/V</td>
</tr>
</table>

B. Label any chord that might be a secondary dominant according to the
steps outlined on page 259. Label all others with an x.

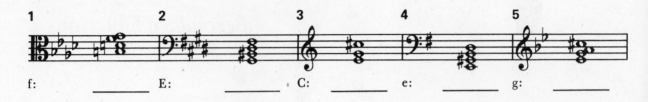

f: _____ E: _____ C: _____ e: _____ g: _____

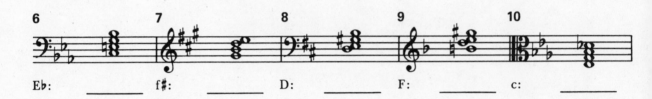

Eb: _____ f#: _____ D: _____ F: _____ c: _____

A: _____ b: _____ d: _____ Bb: _____ G: _____

EXERCISE 16-2

A. Analysis.

    1. Label chords and NCTs. Identify any six-four chords by type. This excerpt contains a set of parallel 5ths in a context that Bach must have found acceptable, since he used them so often in this situation. See if you can find them.

Bach, "Freuet euch, ihr Christen alle"

f:

    2. Label chords and NCTs. Discuss the sequence implied by mm. 5-8. Is the excerpt an example of a period? If so, is it a parallel period or a contrasting period?

Beethoven, Sonata Op. 13, II

3. Label the chords with roman numerals. Thinking in terms of chord roots, find the longest harmonic sequence in this excerpt.

Beethoven, Sonata Op. 2, No. 1, I

4. Label chords and NCTs. Ignore the grace notes in your harmonic and NCT analysis; for example, the E♭5 in m. 1 is an upper neighbor ornamented by the appoggiatura grace note. Comment upon Chopin's use of F♯ and F♮ in this excerpt. Where do they occur? Are they ever in conflict? The form of the excerpt is a (parallel/contrasting) (period/double period).

Chopin, Mazurka Op. 67, No. 2

5. Label chords and NCTs. What is the form of this excerpt? (Note: mm. 1-2 are introductory.)

Beethoven, Quartet Op. 135, III

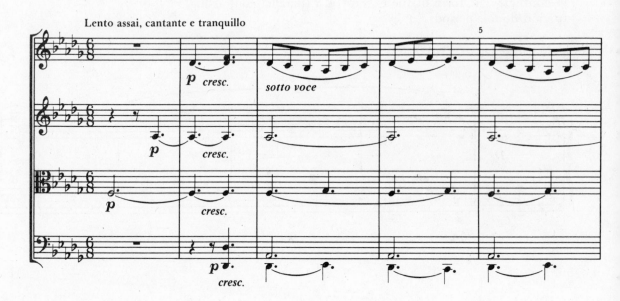

6. Label the chords with roman numerals. Label NCTs in the solo bassoon part only. The note under the fermata in m. 49 represents a V chord. It was at this point that the soloist improvised a cadenza. The conductor waited until he heard the soloist arrive at the G3 (often trilled), at which point he would signal the orchestra to be ready for their entrance in m. 50.

Mozart, Bassoon Concerto K. 191, II

B. For each of the following problems, first analyze the given chord. Next, find a smooth way to lead into the chord. While there are many possibilities, it will often work to use a chord whose root is a P5 above the root of the secondary dominant. Experiment with other relationships also. Then resolve each chord properly, taking special care with the leading tone and 7th resolutions. Analyze all chords.

g: __ __ __   C: __ __ __   G: __ __ $\mathrm{V}^6_5/\mathrm{V}$ E: __ __ __   Ab: __ __ __

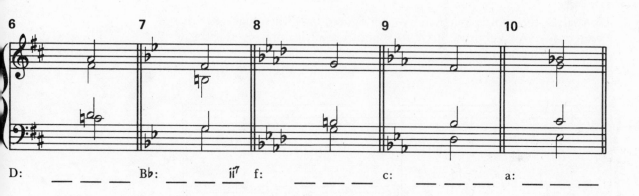

D: __ __ __   Bb: __ __ ii⁷ f: __ __ __   c: __ __ __   a: __ __ __

C. List below each note the secondary V and V⁷ chords that could harmonize that note. You may find it helpful to refer to the charts on page 257.

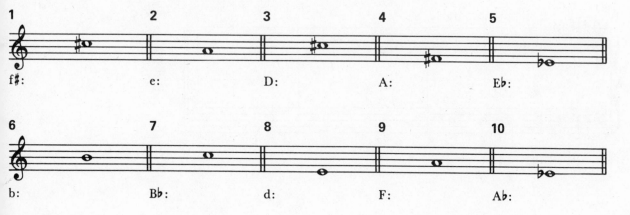

f#:   e: D: A: Eb:

b: Bb: d: F: Ab:

D. Provide roman numerals to show how the first note could be harmonized as a secondary dominant. The second note should be harmonized by the tonicized chord.

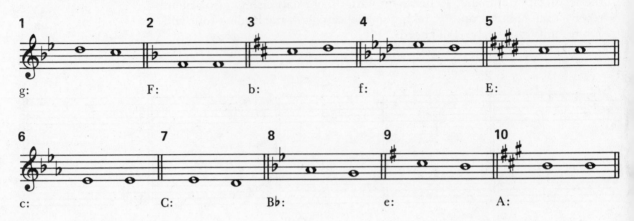

E. Analyze the chords specified by each figured bass, then make an arrangement for SATB chorus. Strive for smooth voice leading, even if this results in a dull soprano line.

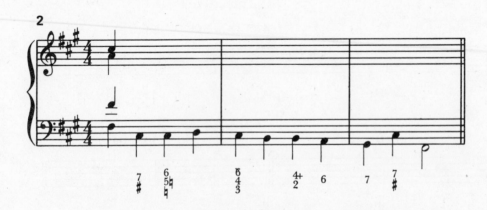

F. Harmonize each chorale phrase for SATB chorus. Include one or more
   secondary dominants in each phrase, and activate the texture with some
   NCTs.

1

Eb: d:

3

C:

4

g:

G. Analyze the harmonies implied by the following soprano/bass framework.
Then make a more interesting version for piano, beginning with the two
measures given below.

H. Continue the example below to make a total of at least eight measures. Include one or more secondary dominants, and end with a PAC. Then score it for four instruments found in your class. Analyze all chords and NCTs.

I. Finish the analysis of the phrase below. This phrase is to serve as the *a* phrase of a longer theme you will compose. The theme will be in the form of a parallel double period. Include at least one secondary dominant.

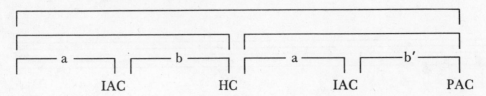

A: (I) (V⁷)   I

CHAPTER 17

Secondary Functions 2

EXERCISE 17-1

A. Review how to spell secondary leading-tone chords (p. 275). Then notate these secondary leading-tone chords in the specified inversion. Include key signatures.

B. Label any chord that would be a secondary leading-tone chord according
to the steps outlined on page 275. Label all others with an *x*.

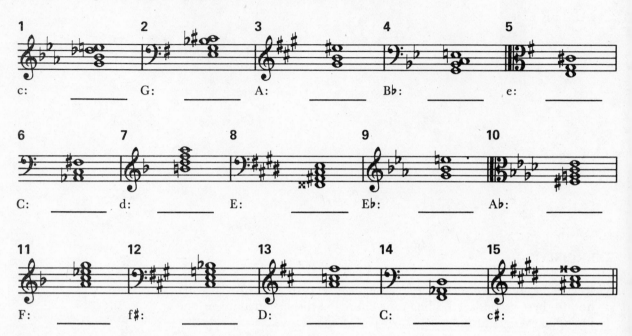

c: _____   G: _____   A: _____   Bb: _____   e: _____

C: _____   d: _____   E: _____   Eb: _____   Ab: _____

F: _____   f#: _____   D: _____   C: _____   c#: _____

EXERCISE 17-2

A. Analysis.

1. In the brilliant and witty concluding passage below, Mozart combines the antecedent and consequent phrases from the beginning of the minuet (marked *a* and *b* in mm. 55-58).

   a. Mark all occurrences of *a* and *b*.

   b. Find where the *b* phrase is used in imitation.

   c. Find inverted (upside down) statements of *a* and *b*.

   d. Find a place where original and inverted statements of *b* occur simultaneously.

   e. Put roman numerals in the blanks provided. NCTs are in parentheses.

Mozart, String Quartet K. 464, II

2. Label the chords with roman numerals (the Italian augmented sixth chord in m. 4 will be discussed in Chapter 23). Use your imagination, and your ear, in analyzing the last chord in m. 2.

Schumann, "Die Löwenbraut," Op. 31, No. 1

3. Label chords and NCTs. (An optional piano accompaniment is omitted from the example.) What is the form of this excerpt?

Brahms, "Und gehst du über den Kirchhof," Op. 44

4. Analyze chords and NCTs. Find two circle-of-fifths progressions that
contain more than four chords. What is the form of this excerpt?

Tchaikovsky, "Morning Prayer," Op. 39, No. 1

5. This short song is given here in its entirety. Analyze the chords and NCTs. There are some places where alternative analyses are possible—in m. 1, for example, where the line G♯-F♯-E could be analyzed as chord tones or as passing tones. Think of two analyses for the second chord in m. 11, one of them being a secondary function.

Schumann, "Aus meinen Thränen spriessen," Op. 48, No. 2

B. For each of these problems, first analyze and resolve the given chord,
being especially careful with the chord 7th and the leading tone. Then
find a smooth way to lead into the given chord. Analyze all chords.

C: ___ ___ ___   D: ___ ___ ___   A: ___ ___ ___   Eb: ___ ___ ___   Bb: ___ ___ ___

E: ___ ___ ___   c: ___ ___ ___   f: ___ ___ ___   g: ___ ___ ___   F: ___ ___ ___

C. Analyze the harmonies specified by each figured bass, and make an arrangement for SATB chorus. Try to use smooth voice leading, even at the
expense of an interesting soprano line.

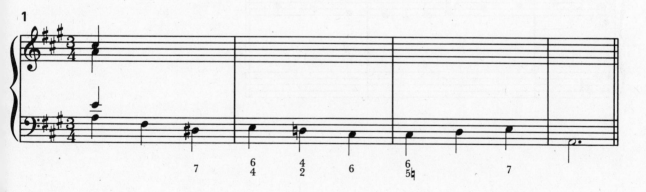

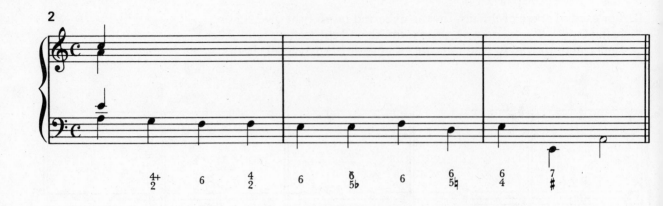

2

$$\begin{array}{ccccccccc} \frac{4+}{2} & 6 & \frac{4}{2} & 6 & \frac{6}{5\flat} & 6 & \frac{6}{5\natural} & \frac{6}{4} & \frac{7}{\#} \end{array}$$

D. Harmonize each of these chorale phrases for SATB chorus. Include at least one secondary leading-tone chord or incorporate some other aspect discussed in this chapter in each harmonization.

1 F:

2 a:

3 F:

E. Each item below contains two versions of the same excerpt, one of them in a simple texture and one more elaborate. Continue the simple texture first, including some aspect of harmony discussed in this chapter. Then continue the elaboration, using your simple version as a framework. Label chords and NCTs.

1a.

1b.

F. Compose a setting of the following poem for chorus (three, four, or five parts) or for solo voice with piano accompaniment. Use at least one secondary leading-tone chord and one deceptive resolution of a secondary dominant. Try to put your special harmonic effects at appropriate places in the text. (Use either or both stanzas.)

> A bird came down the walk;
> He did not know I saw;
> He bit an angle-worm in halves
> And ate the fellow raw.
>
> And then he drank a dew
> From a convenient grass,
> And then hopped sidewise to the wall
> To let a beetle pass.
>
> —From "A bird came down the walk" by Emily Dickinson.

CHAPTER 18

*Modulations Using
Diatonic Common Chords*

EXERCISE 18-1

A. Name the relative key in each case.

1. G♭ ____   **6.** d ____

2. A ____   **7.** F♯ ____

3. e ____   **8.** c♯ ____

4. g ____   **9.** A♭ ____

5. C♯ ____   **10.** a♭ ____

B. Name all the keys closely related to the given key. Be sure to use upper case for major, lower case for minor.

1. b ____ ____ ____ ____ ____

2. e♭ ____ ____ ____ ____ ____

3. G ____ ____ ____ ____ ____

4. B ____ ____ ____ ____ ____

5. F ____ ____ ____ ____ ____

6. f♯ ____ ____ ____ ____ ____

C. Name the relationship in each case (enharmonically equivalent; parallel; relative and closely related; closely related; foreign).

1. D/e _____   **6.** A♭/C♭ _____

2. e♭/G♭ _____   **7.** C♯/D♭ _____

3. A/a _____   **8.** g♯/c♯ _____

4. d♯/G _____   **9.** a♭/b♭ _____

5. B♭/F _____   **10.** c/E♭ _____

EXERCISE 18-2

A. Analysis.

    1. Label chords and NCTs in this chorale, which is presented in its entirety. Which two phrases are very similar melodically? What portion of these phrases is harmonized similarly? What chord is emphasized in the first half of the second of these two phrases?

Bach, "Uns ist ein Kindlein heut' geborn"

162

2. This example, also a complete chorale, is in g minor, although it ends
with a major triad (the "Picardy third"). Label chords and NCTs.
Notice how often the melody follows an arch contour (inverted in the
second phrase). Bracket those arch contours in the melody. If you find
any similar contours in the bass, bracket them also.

Bach, "Jesu, der du meine Seele"

3. Label the chords with roman numerals. How do the pickup notes at the beginning of the excerpt help smooth the return to the first key when the repeat is taken?

Mozart, Sonata K. 330, II

4. Listen to this song all the way through. Then list every tonality that is touched upon in the song, either by simple tonicization or by modulation. Which (other than tonic) is referred to again at the end of the song? Decide upon one or two tonalities (other than tonic) that represent modulations rather than tonicizations. Then label all chords with roman numerals.

Schumann, "Wenn ich in deine Augen seh'," Op. 48, No. 4

Wenn ich in dei - ne Au - gen seh', so schwin-det all' mein Leid und

Weh;   doch wenn ich küs - se dei - nen Mund, so werd'ich ganz und gar ge -

sund. Wenn ich mich lehn' an dei - ne Brust, kommt's ü - ber ruich wie Him - mels-

lust; doch wenn du sprichst: Ich lie - be dich, so muss ich wei - nen bit - ter-

lich.

5. This excerpt begins in A♭ and ends in g minor, modulating through yet another key in the process. Label all chords, and label the NCTs in the vocal part. The German augmented sixth chord in m. 49 will be discussed in a later chapter.

Mozart, Marriage of Figaro, K. 492, "Voi che sapete"

6. Label the chords with roman numerals. In an Alberti bass accompaniment, such as the left hand in this example, the bass note for each chord is usually considered to be the lowest note struck. So in m. 9 the only *bass* notes are D and C♯.

Beethoven, Sonata Op. 10, No. 3, II

B. Fill in the name of the new key on the second line of each exercise.

1. e: i   ii^{o6} V$^4_2$ i^6 iv^6

             ___ :   i^6 V$^4_2$ i^6 ii^{o6} V^7 i

2. D: I   V   I^6 vii^{o6}

             ___ :   ii^{o6} i$^6_4$ V   i
                                   V

3. F: I   vii^{o6} I^6 vi

             ___ :   ii   vii^{o6} I   V$^6_5$ I

4. g: i   V$^6_5$ V$^4_2$/iv   iv^6 V   i^6

                          ___ :   iv^6 ii^{o6} V^7 i

5. b: i   ii$^{ø4}_{2}$ V$^6_5$ i   VI   iv^6

                          ___ :   ii^6 I$^6_4$ V^7 I
                                             V

6. E♭:   I   ii^6 V   vi

             ___ :   iv   ii$^{ø6}_5$ V   VI   iv   V   i

7. A: I   V$^4_3$ I^6 V^6

             ___ :   IV^6 V$^6_5$ i   ii$^{ø6}_5$ i$^6_4$ V^7 i

8. c: i   V^7 VI   iv

             ___ :   vi   IV^6 I$^6_4$ ii$^6_5$ V   I

169

C. List the diatonic triads that could serve as common chords between each pair of keys. In minor keys, assume the usual chord qualities: i, ii°, III, iv, V, VI, vii°.

ex. First key, C: I   iii   V   vi
    Triads: C   e   G   a
    Second key, G: IV   vi   I   ii

1. First key, E:
   Triads:
   Second key, f♯:

2. First key, D♭:
   Triads:
   Second key, G♭:

3. First key, c:
   Triads:
   Second key, B♭:

4. First key, f:
   Triads:
   Second key, A♭:

5. First key, B:
   Triads:
   Second key, F♯:

6. First key, A♭:
   Triads:
   Second key, B♭:

D. Choose two of the progressions from Part B. Arrange one for SATB chorus and the other for SAB chorus. Activate the texture with NCTs and/or arpeggiations. Arrange the metric and rhythmic structure so that the last chord comes on a strong beat. Label chords and NCTs.

E. Harmonize the following chorale tunes for SATB chorus.

   1. In the first phrase, modulate from i to III. The second phrase should return to i.

   2. Modulate from I to vi in phrase 1. Return to I in phrase 2.

F. Analyze the chords specified by this figured bass, and then make an arrangement for SATB chorus.

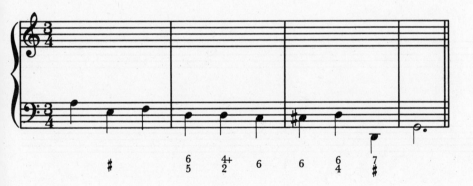

G. Continue this soprano/bass framework, analyzing the implied harmonies. Phrase 1 (mm. 1-4) should end with a HC in f. Phrase 2 (mm. 5-8) should end with a PAC in A♭. The resulting form is a modulating period. Then arrange for some combination of instruments in your class, filling in as many inner parts as needed. Elaborate your final version with NCTs and arpeggiations.

f: i   vii°⁶   i⁶

H. Compose a double period for some solo instrument with piano accompaniment. As the diagram indicates, the first phrase stays in A, while the second tonicizes (or modulates to) E. Phrase 3 returns briefly to A but turns quickly to D. The fourth phrase returns to A for the final cadence.

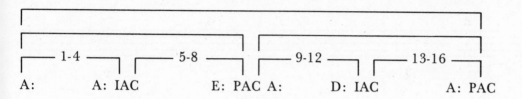

Or, in the larger view:

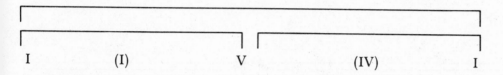

The beginning of phrase 1 is given below. Compose the soprano/bass framework first.

I. Using a text of your own choosing, compose a passage for chorus (three or four parts). If in major, it should have a tonal scheme of I-vi-I-ii-I. If in minor, use i-VI-i-iv-i.

CHAPTER 19

Some Other Modulatory Techniques

EXERCISE 19-1

A. Analysis. (Note: Some of the modulations below may be of the diatonic common-chord type.)

   1. a. What three keys are implied in this excerpt?

      b. How would you explain the modulations?

      c. Continue the two-voice reduction below the score, but avoid the change of register in m. 36.

Beethoven, Sonata Op. 10, No. 1, I

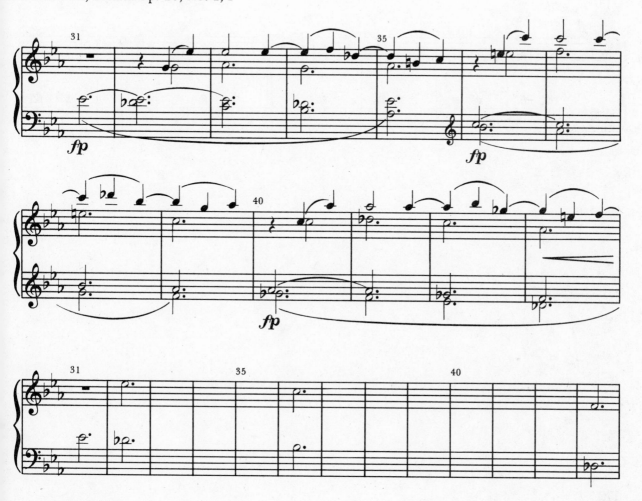

2. There are two modulations in this excerpt. Label chords and NCTs. At what point does Bach not follow the conventions of spacing discussed on page 82? What is achieved by the spacing he uses? Where is there a sonority used in an unusual bass position? How is the reason for this bass position related to the question about the spacing?

Bach, "Warum betrübst du dich"

3. What two keys are found in this excerpt? How are they related? What is the best way to describe the modulation?

Schubert, "Valse sentimentale," Op. 50, No. 13

4. Two distantly related keys are found in this passage. Label chords and NCTs.

Schubert, "Auf dem Flusse," Op. 89, No. 7

Mit har - ter, star - rer Rin - de hast du dich ü - ber - deckt, liegst

kalt und un - be - weg - lich im San - de — aus - ge - streckt.

5. This excerpt modulates from F major to what other key? Of excerpts 1 through 4, which modulation most closely resembles this one? In what ways? (The chords in mm. 35-36 are labeled for you because some of them involve concepts discussed in later chapters.)

Mozart, Marriage of Figaro, K. 492, "Voi che sapete"

Sen - to un af - fet - to pien di de - sir,

Ch'o - ra è di - let - to, ch'o - ra è mar - tir.

i Ger^{+6} V

Ge - lo, e poi sen - to l'al - ma av-vam - par,

B. Analyze the harmonies implied by this soprano/bass framework. Add an
alto part to create a three-part texture. Embellish the texture with a few
NCTs, including a 4-3 suspension. Identify the modulatory technique used.

C. Analyze the implied harmonies, and then add alto and tenor parts. Enliven
the texture with NCTs and/or arpeggiations. Identify the modulatory
technique used.

D. Use the framework below as the basis for a repeated period. The second
   phrase should begin and end in D major (phrase modulation). Compose a
   first ending that modulates back to F using some modulatory technique
   discussed in this chapter. Include NCTs and arpeggiations in your final
   version. Score for piano or some combination of instruments found in
   your class.

E. The framework below is also to be used as the basis for a repeated period for piano (or other instruments). The first phrase is in E♭ and the second should be a sequential repetition of the first, in A♭. Write out the repeat of phrases 1-2. Use more embellishments in the repeat than you used in the first eight measures.

CHAPTER 20

Binary and Ternary Forms

EXERCISE 20-1

A. Diagram this excerpt down to the phrase level and name the form. Assume all phrases are four measures long. Also, answer the following questions:

1. Where is there a vii$^{\o 7}$ over a tonic pedal point?

2. What chord is the basis of mm. 9-12?

3. Label the chords in mm. 13-16.

Mozart, *Eine kleine Nachtmusik*, K. 525, II

B. Name the form of this piece (do not diagram phrases and cadences). Watch
out for written-out repeats. Also, do or answer the following:

1. Label the chords in mm. 5-8.

2. What chord forms the basis of mm. 33-39?

3. Analyze the last chord in m. 34.

4. In what measures does the "boom-chick-chick" accompaniment drop
out?

Chopin, Mazurka Op. 67, No. 3

C. This excerpt is the first part of a scherzo and trio (a scherzo is much like a minuet, only faster). The trio is not shown.

  1. Diagram this scherzo at the phrase level. The key implied by mm. 17-20 is d minor, not A major.

  2. Identify the form. Do not be misled by the written-out repeat in mm. 9-16—this is a two-reprise form.

  3. Find two examples of chromatic mediant relationships.

Beethoven, Violin Sonata Op. 24, III

D. Diagram this piece down to the phrase level and name the form. Also, answer the following questions:

1. Where is a sequence involving both hands? Bracket it.

2. What does the G♯4 in m. 6 accomplish?

3. What material in mm. 10-22 is obviously derived from mm. 1-9?

March from the *Notebook for Anna Magdalena Bach*

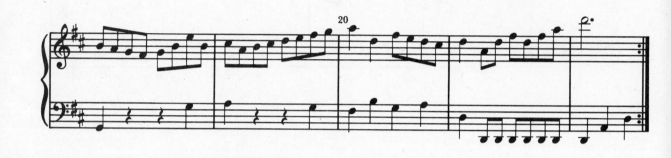

E. This excerpt, the final movement of a piano sonata, is a minuet and trio, although Haydn did not label it as such.

1. Diagram phrases and cadences, treating the minuet and trio as separate pieces. Be sure to play or listen to the music, because some of the returns are disguised. (A melodically varied return of phrase *a* is still labeled phrase *a*, not phrase *a'*.)

2. Name the forms of the minuet and of the trio.

3. In performance, the trio is followed by a return to the minuet (although the repeats are omitted), ending at the fermata. What is the form of the movement as a whole?

4. Find the one phrase in this movement that is not four measures long, and compare it to its earlier four-measure version. How does Haydn extend this phrase?

5. Provide roman numerals for the following chords:

   a. _____ m. 17, beats 1-2 (in E♭)

   b. _____ m. 19, beat 3 (in E♭)

   c. _____ m. 35, beat 3 (in A♭)

   d. _____ m. 44 (in A♭)

   e. _____ m. 46, beat 3 (in A♭)

Haydn, Piano Sonata No. 38, III

Da Capo sin al segno 🎵

Mode Mixture

EXERCISE 21-1

A. Notate these chords in the specified inversions. Include key signatures.

A: ii$^{\varnothing4}_{2}$ F: vii$^{\text{o}7}$ D♭: i$^{6}_{4}$ C: ♭VI   E: ii$^{\text{o}6}$

A♭: vii$^{\text{o}6}_{5}$ E♭: iv   f♯: I   D: ♭III   G: iv^{6}

B. Label these chords. Include inversion symbols.

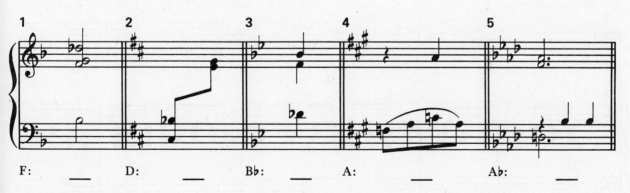

F: ___   D: ___   B♭: ___   A: ___   A♭: ___

C. Analysis.

   1. Label the chords with roman numerals. NCTs have been put in parentheses (other interpretations are possible). Which chord could be considered an example of secondary mode mixture?

Bach, "Herr Jesu Christ, wahr'r Mensch und Gott"

C:

   2. Label the chords and NCTs. Circle the roman numerals of any borrowed chords.

Schumann, "Ich grolle nicht," Op. 48, No. 7

3. Label the chords, circling the roman numerals of any borrowed chords. Label the cadence type.

Brahms, Symphony No. 3, Op. 90, II

4. In the passage below, Mozart uses mode mixture twice to move from
E major to the very distant key of c minor, and then uses mode mixture
twice more to return to E major. Label all chords, including the common-
chord modulations from E to c and back. (Remember that the bass voice
is always the lowest sounding voice, so that the bass note in m. 221, for
example, is the cello G, not the piano E♭.)

Mozart, Piano Trio K. 542, I

5. This excerpt modulates from A♭ to some other key and then back to
  A♭. Label all chords and NCTs.

Schubert, Impromptu Op. 90, No. 1

D. Part writing. Analyze the chords implied by the soprano/bass framework.
Then fill in alto and tenor parts. Be sure to use the specified mode mixture.

1. Include a ii$^{\emptyset 6}_{5}$.

2. Include a iv^6 and a ii$^{\emptyset 4}_{3}$.

E. The first two phrases of a chorale melody are given below. A bass line is included for the first phrase. Complete the four-part texture, including in the second phrase a modulation to B♭ and a borrowed iv⁶ chord. Label all chords and circle the roman numeral of the borrowed chord. Activate the texture with NCTs and/or arpeggiations.

F. Analyze the harmonies specified by the following figured bass, and then make an arrangement for SATB chorus. This passage does modulate.

G. Arrange the first modulation below for SAB chorus and the second one
   for SATB chorus. Activate the textures with NCTs and/or arpeggiations.
   Arrange the metric and rhythmic structure so that the last chord comes
   on a strong beat. Label chords and NCTs.

1. D: I   V I^6 vi iv^6

   F: ii^6 V^4_2 I^6 II^6_5 I^6_4 V   I

2. F: I vii^{o6}_5 I^6 V^6_5 I vii^{o4}_3/IV iv^6

   bb: i^6 iv i^6_4 V   i

H. Use the framework below as the basis for the beginning of a passage that
   starts in F major and modulates to D♭ major by means of mode mixture.
   Score for piano or for some combination of instruments in your class.

205

CHAPTER 22

The Neapolitan Chord

EXERCISE 22-1

A. Label each chord. Include inversions, if appropriate.

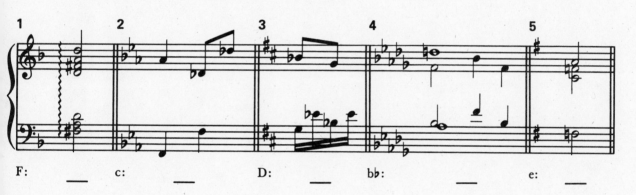

F: _____   c: _____   D: _____   bb: _____   e: _____

D: _____   E: _____   d: _____   f#: _____   Ab: _____

B. Notate each chord. Include key signatures.

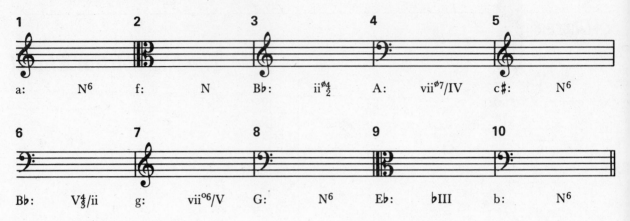

1
a: N^6

2
f: N

3
B♭:   ii°4/2

4
A: vii°7/IV

5
c♯:   N^6

6
B♭:   V4/3/ii

7
g: vii°6/V

8
G: N^6

9
E♭:   ♭III

10
b: N^6

C. Analysis.

1. Label chords and NCTs.

Chopin, Prelude Op. 28, No. 20

2. Label the chords in this excerpt.

Beethoven, Sonata Op. 27, No. 2, I

3. At this point in Schubert's famous "Erlkönig," the evil personality of the title character is finally expressed, with the help of the Neapolitan triad. Label the chords.

Schubert, "Erlkönig," Op. 1

d:

"Ich lie - be dich, mich reizt dei - ne schö - ne Ge - stalt; und

bist du nicht wil - lig, so brauch ich Ge - walt."

4. At the end of the song, the father's frantic ride comes to an end, and
we hear the Neapolitan again. Label the chords.

Schubert, "Erlkönig," Op. 1

5. Mode mixture is involved in this excerpt in modulations to the key of the Neapolitan and back again. Label all chords, including common chords for both modulations.

Beethoven, Rondo, Op. 51, No. 1

D. For each exercise, provide the correct key signature and notate the specified chords preceding and following the N⁶. Use the given three- or four-part texture in each case.

b: iv   N⁶   V   e: VI   N⁶   V⁴₂   c: iv   N⁶ $\underset{V}{\underbrace{i^6_4 \quad V}}$ f♯:   i⁶   N⁶   V⁴₂

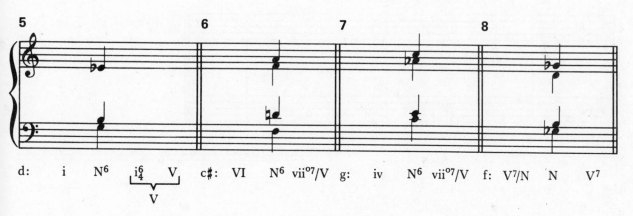

d: i   N⁶ $\underset{V}{\underbrace{i^6_4 \quad V}}$ c♯:   VI   N⁶   vii°⁷/V   g: iv   N⁶   vii°⁷/V   f: V⁷/N   N   V⁷

E. Analyze the harmonies implied by the soprano/bass framework. Then fill in inner voices to make a four-part texture. Each exercise should contain a Neapolitan chord.

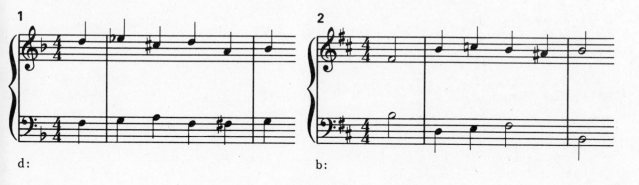

d: b:

213

3

c:

F. Analyze the chords specified by this figured bass, and then make an arrangement for SATB chorus.

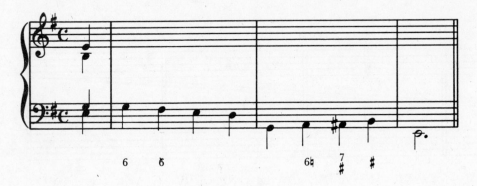

G. Make settings of the following progressions for three or four parts, as specified. Arrange the rhythmic/metric scheme so that the final chord of each progression comes on a strong beat. Activate the texture with arpeggiations and/or NCTs.

1. (4 parts) g: i V i^6 i VI V$^4_2$/N N^6 vii^{o7}/V i$^6_4$ V i

2. (3 parts) e: i V$^4_2$/iv iv^6 i$^6_4$ N^6 V$^4_2$ i^6 vii^{o6} i

3. (4 parts) E♭: I I^6 vi ii V I^6

                                                               d: N^6 vii^{o7}/V i$^6_4$ V^7 i

4. (3 parts) b: i V VI i^6 N^6

                                                               G: IV^6 V$^6_5$ I V I

H. Use the framework below as the first phrase of a three-phrase excerpt
   having the following structure:

b: HC   ∿ f#:   HC   PAC

Phrase 2 modulates to f# minor. Phrase 3 remains in f# minor and contains a Neapolitan triad. After completing the framework, make a more
elaborate version for piano or for some combination of instruments in
your class.

I. Make a setting of the following text or another text of your choice for three-part chorus. Include in your setting examples of the following:

Neapolitan triad

Mode mixture

Common-chord modulation

Your composition should begin and end in the same key. Be sure to include a harmonic analysis.

A storm of white petals,
Buds throwing open baby fists
Into hands of broad flowers.

—From "The Year," in *Cornhuskers* by Carl Sandburg, copyright 1918 by Holt, Rinehart and Winston, Inc.; renewed 1946 by Carl Sandburg. Reprinted by permission of Harcourt Brace & Company.

CHAPTER 23

Augmented Sixth Chords 1

EXERCISE 23-1

A. Label each chord, using inversion symbols where appropriate.

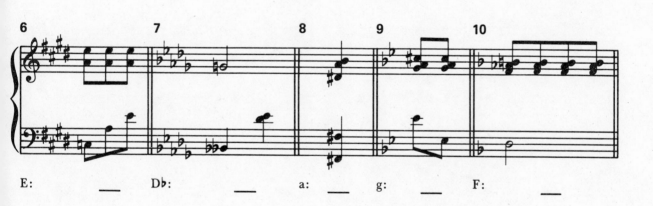

B. Notate each chord in close position. Augmented sixth chords should be in their customary bass position (♭6̂ in the bass). Include key signatures.

1 Bb: Fr+6   2 d: N6   3 bb: Ger+6   4 Ab: It+6   5 B: ii°6/5

6 f#: It+6   7 A: Ger+6   8 c: Fr+6   9 G: vii°7/vi   10 e: Ger+6

C. Label the chords in each example below. Also, discuss the details of the resolution of each augmented sixth chord. Do $\sharp\hat{4}$ and $\flat\hat{6}$ follow their expected resolutions to $\hat{5}$? How are parallel 5ths avoided in the Ger^{+6} resolution(s)?

1. Measures 2-5 of this excerpt are in d minor, although the key of VI (B♭) is strongly tonicized in mm. 2-3 (the second chord in m. 2 should be analyzed as a secondary function of VI). Common-chord modulations to two other keys occur in mm. 5-11.

Schumann, "Sehnsucht," Op. 51, No. 1

hält mich der Nord, __ ich er - rei - che sie nicht. O die Schran - ken so eng, __ und die

Welt __ so weit,

2. This excerpt begins and ends in g minor, but it contains modulations to
two other keys (or tonicizations of two other chords). How do those
keys relate to the "parent" tonality of g minor?

Schumann, "Die beiden Grenadiere," Op. 49, No. 1

wohl ob der kläg - li - chen Kun - de. Der Ei - ne sprach: "Wie weh wird

mir, wie brennt mei - ne al - te Wun - de!" Der An - dre sprach: "Das Lied ist

aus, auch ich möcht' mit dir ster - ben, doch hab' ich Weib und

Kind zu Haus, die oh - ne mich ver - der - ben." "Was schert mich Weib,

3. This excerpt begins in C major and modulates. Where is there a 9-8 suspension?

Haydn, Quartet Op. 74, No. 3, II

4. This excerpt modulates to the dominant, passing through another key on the way. The first chord in m. 8 is spelled enharmonically (imagine a G♮ instead of the F✗). Be sure to analyze a chord on beat 2 of m. 8.

Schumann, Tragödie, Op. 136, No. 3

5. The slow tempo of this theme allows some measures to contain several
chords. In the first measure, for instance, each bass note is harmonized
by a new chord, with the exception of the B2. Discuss the various uses
of the pitch class G♯/A♭ in this excerpt.

🎧 Beethoven, String Trio Op. 9, No. 3, II

D. Supply the missing voices for each fragment below. All are four-part textures.

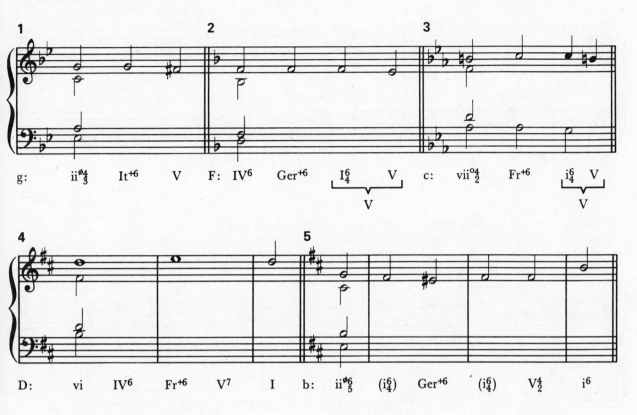

1 g: ii⌀⁴₃ It⁺⁶ V   2 F: IV⁶ Ger⁺⁶ I⁶₄ V   3 c: vii°⁴₂ Fr⁺⁶ i⁶₄ V
                                              └─V─┘   └─V─┘

4 D: vi IV⁶ Fr⁺⁶ V⁷ I   5 b: ii⌀⁶₅ (i⁶₄) Ger⁺⁶ (i⁶₄) V⁴₂ i⁶

E. Complete these harmonizations, adding one or two inner voices, as specified.

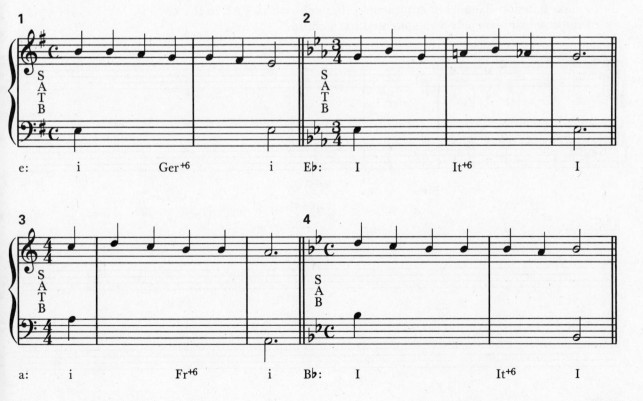

1 e: i Ger⁺⁶ i   2 Eb: I It⁺⁶ I

3 a: i Fr⁺⁶ i   4 Bb: I It⁺⁶ I

227

F. Analyze the harmonies specified by this figured bass, and then make an arrangement for SATB chorus.

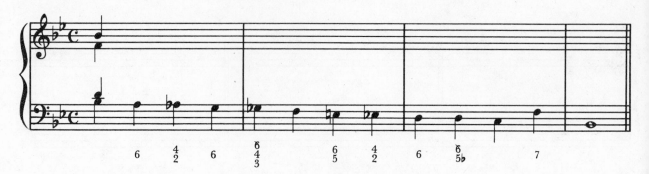

G. Analyze the harmonies implied by this soprano/bass framework, being sure to include an It⁺⁶. Then fill in the inner voices, following good voice-leading procedures. There are no NCTs in the bass and soprano lines.

H. Given below are mm. 1-2 of a four-measure phrase. Continue the passage to make a period (parallel or contrasting) that ends with a PAC in the key of the dominant. Include an augmented sixth chord.

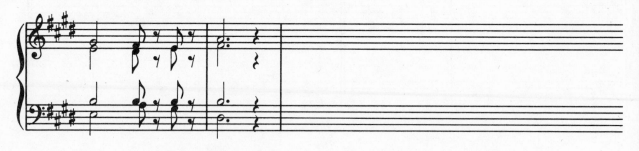

I. Make a setting of the following text or another text of your choice for three-part chorus. Include in your setting examples of the following:

Neapolitan triad

Mode mixture

Secondary function

Augmented sixth chord

Remember to include tempo indication and dynamic markings.

Two roads diverged in a wood, and I —
I took the one less traveled by,
And that has made all the difference.

—From "The Road Not Taken," by Robert Frost. From *The Poetry of Robert Frost*, edited by Edward Connery Lathem. Copyright 1916, © 1969 by Henry Holt and Company, Inc. Copyright 1944 by Robert Frost. Reprinted by permission of Henry Holt and Company, Inc.

CHAPTER 24

Augmented Sixth Chords 2

EXERCISE 24-1

A. Label the chords in the keys indicated.

g: ___ ___   b: ___ ___   A♭: ___ ___ ___   G: ___ ___   f♯: ___ ___

f: ___ ___   d: ___ ___   E♭: ___ ___ ___   E: ___ ___   B♭: ___ ___

1. Label the chords in this example. Measures 10-12 could be analyzed in terms of secondary functions or as a modulation.

Tchaikovsky, "The Nurse's Tale," Op. 39, No. 19

2. In a number of his works Scriabin used the chord found at the end of the first measure. Label the chords.

Scriabin, *Tragic Poem,* Op. 34

3. This excerpt will give you practice with both alto and tenor clefs. Label
all chords and NCTs.

Schubert, String Trio D. 471

4. This example begins in A and modulates. Label the chords.

Schumann, "Novellette," Op. 21, No. 7 (simplified texture)

f#:

5. Label the chords.

Beethoven, Violin Sonata Op. 23, III

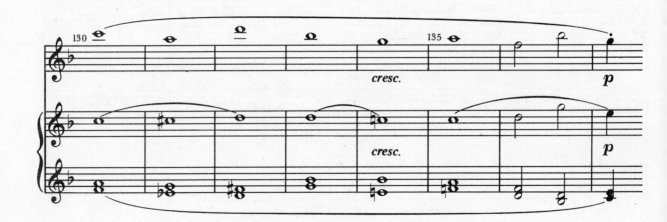

CHAPTER 25

Enharmonic Spellings and Enharmonic Modulations

EXERCISE 25-1

A. Analyze the given chord. Then show any possible enharmonic reinterpretation(s) of that chord, keeping the same key signature. The enharmonic reinterpretation should involve a new key, not just an enharmonically equivalent key (like g♯ and a♭). Number 1 is supplied as an example.

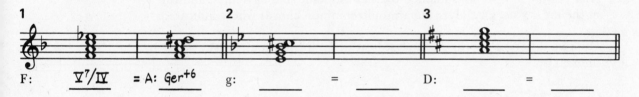

F: $\underline{\text{V}^7/\text{IV}}$ = A: $\underline{\text{Ger}^{+6}}$ g: ___ = ___   D: ___ = ___

B♭: ___ = ___ = ___ = ___   F♯: ___ = ___

B. Each of the following short passages contains an enharmonic modulation. Analyze each passage after playing it slowly at the piano and listening for the point of modulation. Do not try to analyze these passages without hearing them.

1

2

3

C. Analyze the progressions implied by these soprano and bass lines, and fill in the inner voices. Analyze enharmonic common chords where indicated.

Use two different chords on the last beat of m. 2 and the first beat of m. 3 in exercise 1.

D. Compose short passages similar to those in Part B. The given chord is to serve as the common chord in an enharmonic modulation. (Hint: As you sketch out your progression, notate the given chord first. Then find satisfactory ways to lead into and away from that chord.)

1. G to B. Common chord: V^7/IV in G.

2. b to Bb. Common chord: $vii°^7/iv$ in b.

3. Bb to E. Common chord: $vii°{}^6_5$ in Bb.

4. E to F. Common chord: Ger^{+6} in E.

E. Analysis. Be sure to play as much as you can of each excerpt.

1. This passage modulates from f♯ minor to A♭ major by way of E major. The bass notes are found above the *"Ped."* markings—the other notes in the bass clef are arpeggiations into inner voices. Label all of the chords, including common chords for both modulations.

Chopin, Nocturne Op. 27, No. 1

238

2. This excerpt begins in g minor. Label all the chords.

Beethoven, Sonata Op. 13, I

3. This excerpt begins in B major and ends in E major, but there are modulations to B♭ and D♭ along the way. Label all of the chords, and analyze common chords for each modulation.

Schubert, Piano Sonata in B♭, D. 960, I

4. The next excerpt is quite challenging. Label both chords and NCTs. You might find it helpful to label the chords with pop symbols before assigning roman numerals.

Haydn, Quartet Op. 76, No. 6, II

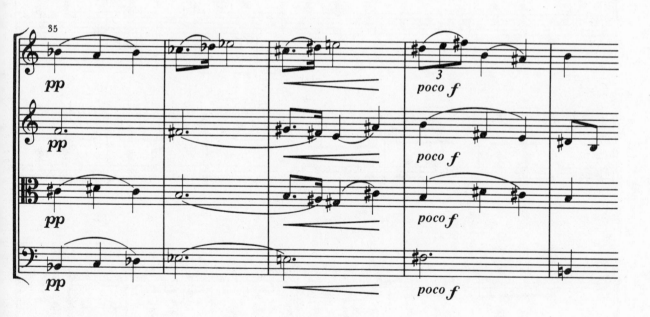

5. This dance modulates from D♭ to A and back again. Although both modulations involve enharmonicism, only one of them is a true enharmonic modulation—the other uses enharmonic spellings for convenience.

   a. Label all the chords, including two common-chord modulations.

   b. Label the enharmonic modulation.

   c. Name the form of this piece.

Schubert, Originaltänze, Op. 9 (D. 365), No. 14

F. Use mm. 31-34 of Part E, number 4, as the first phrase of an eight-measure
   parallel period. The second phrase should include an enharmonic modulation
   to a foreign key.

G. Compose the beginning of a song with piano accompaniment, using a text of your choice. Include two enharmonic modulations, one of them using a Ger^{+6} chord, the other a diminished seventh chord.

CHAPTER 26

Further Elements of the Harmonic Vocabulary

EXERCISE 26-1

A. In each fragment below, analyze the given chord. Then notate the specified chord in such a way that it leads smoothly into the given chord with acceptable voice leading. Some of the problems use a five-part texture for simpler voice leading.

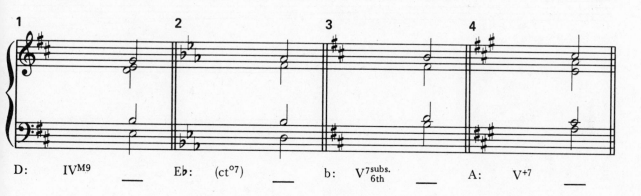

D: IV^{M9} ___   E♭: (ct^{o7}) ___   b: V$^{7subs.}_{6th}$ ___   A: V^{+7} ___

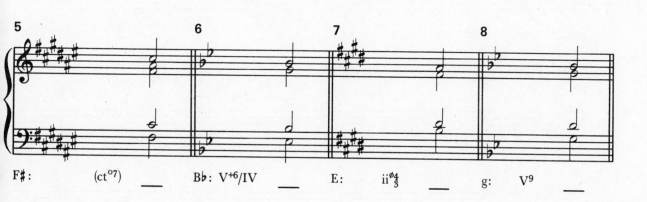

F♯: (ct^{o7}) ___   B♭: V^{+6}/IV ___   E: ii$^{ø4}_{3}$ ___   g: V^{9} ___

B. Compose four short passages for piano, each one making use of a different progression from Part A. The half-note durations do not need to be retained, but use the same voice leading.

C. Analysis. Throughout this section highlight (using arrows or whatever is convenient) any occurrences of the chords discussed in this chapter.

1. Label chords and NCTs.

Schumann, *Humoresque,* Op. 20

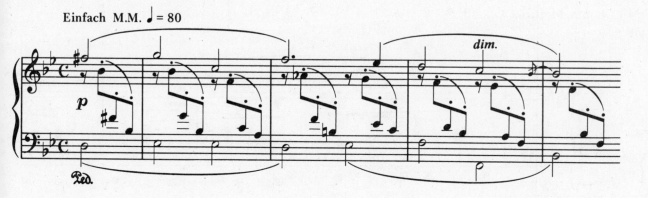

2. a. Analyze this excerpt in f minor throughout. One of the chords is best
   analyzed as a chord with an added 6th.

   b. Put parentheses around NCTs and be prepared to discuss them.

   c. Diagram the phrase structure and label the form. Assume four-
   measure phrases.

Chopin, Mazurka, Op. 63, No. 2

3. The excerpt below is written for barbershop quartet. The treble clef part sounds an octave lower, and the melody is given to the second tenor (the bottom voice in the treble clef). Music for barbershop quartet frequently uses ct^{o7} chords, and you will find some in this excerpt, including one that embellishes a secondary dominant. Label all chords and NCTs, analyzing in A♭ throughout.

Ayer (arr. by Campbell), "Oh! You Beautiful Doll"

4. Harmonic sequences occupy most of this excerpt. Find the two sequences, and bracket each occurrence of the sequential patterns. If it is possible to do so, label the chords in the sequences with roman numerals, perhaps in terms of shifting tonalities. Discuss briefly the large-scale harmonic/melodic function of each sequence. In other words, just what does each sequence accomplish harmonically and melodically?

Schumann, "Die Löwenbraut," Op. 31, No. 1

5. This familiar excerpt is easier to listen to than to analyze. The transpositions do not make the analysis any easier—clarinets in A and horns
in F—nor do the four clefs in use. Do your best with the score (after all,
conductors face this sort of problem every day), then check your work
with the piano arrangement that follows the excerpt.

Tchaikovsky, Symphony No. 6, Op. 74, I

6. Label with roman numerals the two chords in this excerpt that are the most important structurally. The other chords are simultaneities connecting the structural chords. Label their roots. If any of these chords imply fleeting tonicizations, indicate this with roman numerals. The chord in m. 2 could be heard as a g triad with raised *and* lowered 5th (G-Bb-Db-D#), since the Eb ascends chromatically to E, as we would expect D# to do. Find another chord in this passage that could be interpreted similarly.

Wagner, *Siegfried,* Act I (piano-vocal score)

7. In some ways this excerpt pushes traditional harmony toward its limits, especially through its disregard for conventional resolutions of dissonance. Nevertheless, the entire passage can be analyzed reasonably well in traditional terms. Label all of the chords. Which portion of the excerpt is the most unconventional in terms of dissonance treatment?

Grieg, "The Mountain Maid," Op. 67, No. 2

Tonal Harmony in the Late Nineteenth Century

EXERCISE 27-1

A. Examine the first twenty-five measures of the opening of *Tannhäuser*, given below, and do the following:

1. The opening eight measures show rather traditional harmonic function. Analyze these measures, using roman numerals (do all work on the music).

2. The following eight measures, which may also be analyzed with roman numerals, show less traditional harmonic movement. Cite at least three instances in which this is true (show measure number).

   a. _____

   b. _____

   c. _____

3. Analyze the sequence that begins at m. 17 and continues through m. 21.

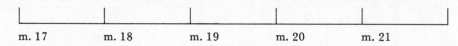

m. 17   m. 18   m. 19   m. 20   m. 21

Use pop symbols, roman numerals, or a mixture of both, whichever seems appropriate. Circle those chords which are most strongly tonicized. How is such tonicization accomplished?

Wagner, *Tannhäuser*, Prelude to Act I (piano reduction)

B. Analyze the following chromatic sequences; then continue each as indicated.

Select one of the above sequence patterns to serve as the basis for a piano composition. You may wish to create a melody over the background of block chords, or perhaps modify the texture of the harmonies themselves. Nonessential or embellishing chords may be inserted within the sequence for the purpose of color.

C. Continue the following sequences as indicated. Then select one to serve as the harmonic basis for a piano or vocal composition in the style of one of the post-Romantic composers studied. Strive for contrapuntal interest and smooth voice leading.

D. Examine the following excerpt.

1. The opening key is designated as E major. What is interesting about the structure of the scale which forms the basis for mm. 2 and 3? _____

   _____

   _____

2. Provide roman numeral analysis for m. 2. _____
   In what way does the music in mm. 10-11 suggest more traditional

   treatment of tonality? _____

   _____

3. Describe the modulatory procedure which takes place in mm. 12-13.

   _____

   _____

4. Name the key introduced in m. 14. _____

   What is its relationship to the opening key? _____

5. Name two other keys hinted at between mm. 1 and 14. _____

   and _____ These keys represent what relationship to each

   other and to the opening key? _____

Wolf, "Die ihr schwebet um diese Palmen"

es schlum - mert mein Kind.

Ihr Pal - men

von Beth - le - hem im

E. **1.** Is there a clear tonal center in the opening five bars of the following excerpt? If so, what is it and how is it defined? _____

_____

_____

2. Using pop symbols, name the two sonorities found in mm. 6 and 7.

_____ and _____ In what way could these chords be said to suggest functional harmony in the key of D major which ultimately concludes the excerpt, as well as the piece? _____

_____

3. What roman numerals are used in mm. 9-12 to prepare the cadence in D major?

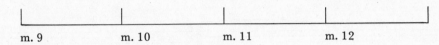

m. 9   m. 10   m. 11   m. 12

Wolf, "Verschwiegene Liebe"

in den Glanz___ hin - ein,___ wer mag sie er - ra - ten, wer

hol - te sie ein?___ Ge -

dan - ken sich wie - gen, die Nacht ist ver - schwie - gen, Ge -

dan - ken sind frei. Er -

F. The first ten measures of *Reverie* may be analyzed with traditional roman numerals (if you watch out for enharmonic respellings). Do so; then comment on reasons for the rather contemporary sound of the piece.

Payne, *Reverie*

_____

_____

_____

_____

_____

G. 1. The following excerpt begins and ends in E major. What is unusual about the manner in which the key is established in mm. 10-13?

_____

_____

_____

2. Label on the music the harmonies found in mm. 14-22. Use pop symbols for your analysis.

3. What five-chord succession within measures 14-22 represents an "omnibus" fragment? _____

4. In what way is the approach to the closing E major harmony unusual?

_____

_____

5. By what means does Fauré make it convincing, nonetheless?

_____

_____

_____

Fauré, "Chanson d'Amour," Op. 27, No. 1 (mm. 10-22)

, *poco* *a* *poco* (ᴖ) *cresc.*

dis,   O   ma   re - belle,   ô   mon cher an - ge,

cresc.

20 *f*   (ᴖ)   (ᴖ) ***p***

Mon en - fer   et mon pa - ra - dis!   J'ai - me tes yeux

mf   ***p***

H. 1. In the *Siegfried* excerpt, analyze one essential harmony for each of the first eleven measures of the excerpt.

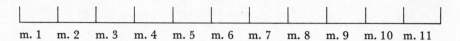

m. 1   m. 2   m. 3   m. 4   m. 5   m. 6   m. 7   m. 8   m. 9   m. 10   m. 11

2. Name at least three keys (including the first one) which are established throughout the course of this excerpt. Show measure numbers.

——————   ——————   ——————

3. Show two instances in which modulation is effected by deceptive resolution, either of chords or of single pitches. Describe the process

that takes place. _____

_____

_____

_____

Wagner, *Siegfried* (Act III, Scene 3)

(feurig, doch zart)

wig zu dei - nem Heil! O Sieg - fried, Herr - li - cher! Hort___ der

Welt! Le - ben der Er - de, la - chen - der

Held!___ Lass', ach, lass'! Las - se von mir!___ Na___ he mir nicht___ mit der

I. **1.** What is unusual about the treatment of tonality in the opening four measures of the Franck prelude? _____

_____

2. Describe the nontraditional treatment of the dominant seventh sonority in mm. 5-9 of the excerpt. _____

_____

3. In what way is the musical style significantly influenced by the treatment of nonharmonic material? Consider both single tones and vertical sonorities. _____

_____

_____

_____

Franck, *Prelude, Aria, and Finale for Piano* (Prelude)

J. The following excerpt is taken from the *Barcarolle,* Op. 17, No. 6, by
Richard Strauss (mm. 21-30).

1. What key is implied by the melody in the opening four bars? _____

2. What means does Strauss employ to negate that tonal implication,

   and indeed, any clear tonal implication? _____

   _____

   _____

   _____

3. Show the underlying harmonic structure of mm. 25-29, using pop
   symbols.

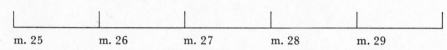

   m. 25   m. 26   m. 27   m. 28   m. 29

4. Within the passage shown above, locate and describe at least three
   examples of deceptive resolution which serve to make the chord
   succession convincing.

   a. _____

   b. _____

   c. _____

R. Strauss, *Barcarolle,* Op. 17, No. 6

seh' ich das säu - len-ge-tra-ge-ne Dach,

und das flim-mern-de Licht___ am Al-ta - ne kün-det mir, dass die Ge-

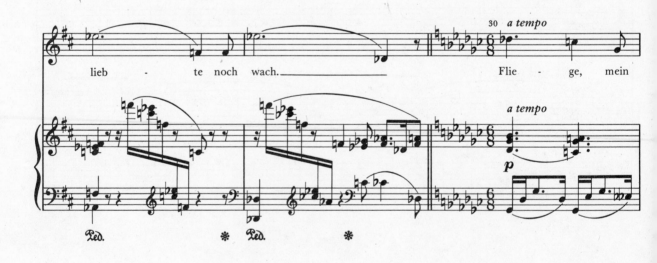

lieb - te noch wach.___ Flie - ge, mein

CHAPTER 28

An Introduction to Twentieth-Century Practices

EXERCISE 28-1

A. Add the appropriate accidentals (or delete the appropriate notes) to create the type of scale asked for.

Mixolydian   Pentatonic

♯4, ♭7   Phrygian

Whole tone   Locrian

B. Using the pentatonic scale of B♭-C-D-F-G, compose five brief melodies, each of which in turn establishes a different one of the above pitches as tonic. (Hint: D is tough. Why?)

1

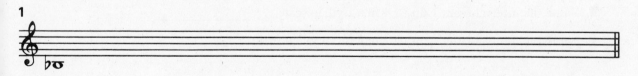

2

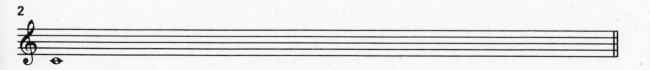

3

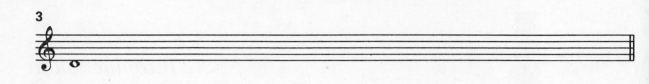

4

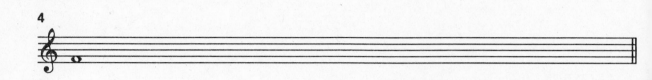

5

C. **1.** All the modes contain a perfect 5th from $\hat{1}$ up to $\hat{5}$ except the

_____ .

2. The three modes that are essentially *minor* in quality are the

_____ , _____ , and _____ .

3. The modal scales that contain a leading tone are the

_____ and _____ .

4. The $\hat{1}$-$\hat{4}$ tetrachord in the Mixolydian scale matches that of the

_____ scale.

5. Likewise, the opening tetrachords of the Aeolian and _____ scale are the same.

6. Those scales containing a major 6th from $\hat{1}$ up to $\hat{6}$ are the

_____ , _____ , _____ , and _____ .

7. Name the interval from $\hat{1}$ up to $\hat{4}$ in a Lydian scale. _____

8. Name the interval from $\hat{4}$ up to $\hat{7}$ in a Mixolydian scale. _____

D. Identify the scale that forms the basis for the following melodies:

1 Moderately

_____

2

_____

3

_____

E. Identify the scale used in the following passages:

1 Allegretto

_____

F. The following examples represent three versions of the principal tune
from Debussy's "Fêtes." For each, identify the mode or scale being used.

Debussy, "Fêtes," from *Nocturnes* (piano reduction)

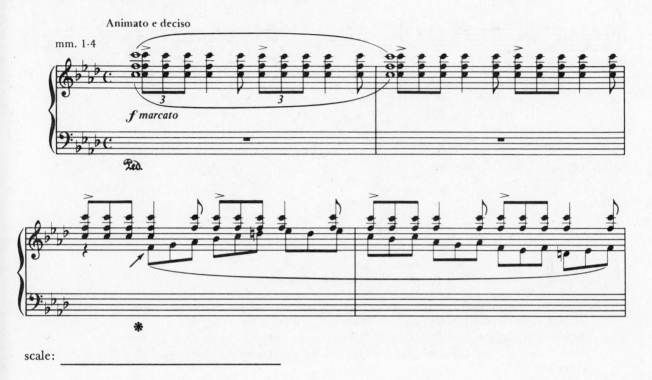

scale: _____

scale: _____

Used by permission of Edward B. Marks Music Co.

mm. 29-32

scale: _____

G. Compose pieces according to the following specifications:

1. Create a melody that contains no intervals other than major or minor 3rds. Use rhythmic interest to keep your melody from sounding like a series of arpeggios. You may find it interesting to analyze the pitches that comprise your finished melody and see if a particular scale pattern emerges.

2. Create a two-voice composition based on a whole-tone scale. You might wish to create a symmetrical relationship between the two voices, or perhaps treat them imitatively. If your composition is for piano, experiment with the wide range of the keyboard.

H. Describe the types of vertical sonorities found in the following examples:

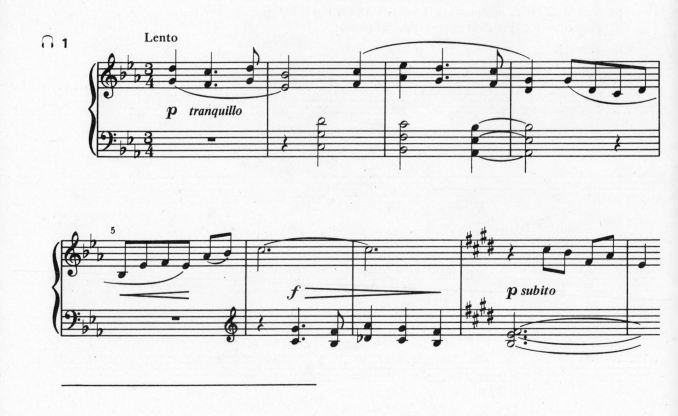

3 Allegro

4 Grave

283

I. Complete the following passages using *strict* parallelism. That is, harmonize each melody note with a chord scored exactly like the preceding one in terms of vertical intervals. Try playing these at the keyboard.

J. Devise completions for the following passages. Include both black and white keys in your solution. Try to maintain stylistic consistency.

1

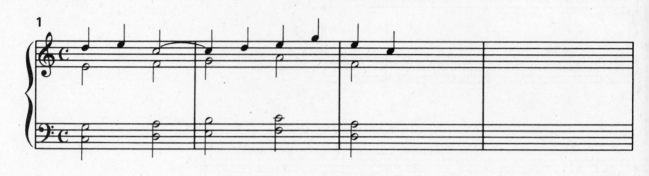

2

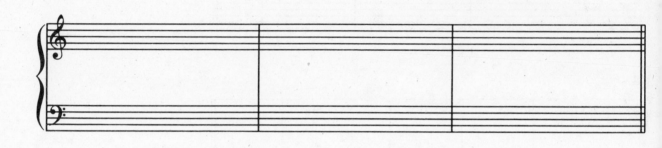

3

K. Compose a brief work for piano employing tall chords, including a few elevenths and thirteenths, in a basically non-tonal context. Include some examples of strict planing.

L. Complete the following passages, using the triad type indicated for each hand. Continue the scoring suggested by the first polychord, using the given outer parts consistently as either roots, 3rds, or 5ths of the sonority.

1

R.H. major, L.H. major

2

R.H. major, L.H. major

3

R.H. major, L.H. minor

4

R.H. major, L.H. minor

5

R.H. minor, L.H. minor

M. Comment on the stylistic features of the following excerpts. Consider
rhythm, texture, pitch choice, and treatment of tonality.

1 Maestoso

_____

_____

_____

begin as rapidly as possible,
then gradually slower

Stravinsky, "Danse russe," from *Petrouchka* (piano reduction)

Stravinsky, "Danse de la foire," from *Petrouchka* (piano reduction)

N. Examine the following étude.

   1. What is interesting about the relationship of the left and right hands throughout the piece? _____

   _____

   2. What is the opening key of the piece? _____

   3. What scale is employed in measures 11-20? _____

   4. In what sense is this scale pattern "violated" in measures 17 and 18?

   _____

   5. In what way does the ending of the piece refer back to the middle

   section? _____

   6. How would you describe the overall form of the piece? _____

   _____

Payne, *Étude*

O. Notate the pitches of the following trichords, as indicated. Where necessary, rearrange each set in *normal order*. For each trichord, give vector analysis.

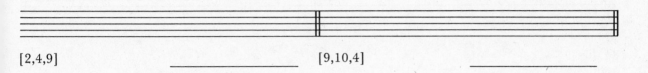

[3,4,9] _____   [6,9,2] _____

[2,4,9] _____   [9,10,4] _____

[1,8,11] _____   [0,5,10] _____

P. For each of the following sonorities, provide (1) vector analysis and (2) name of chord, if appropriate (i.e., polychord, mystic chord, etc.)

_____ _____ _____ _____ _____

_____ _____ _____ _____ _____

Q. **1.** Analyze the intervals in the following twelve-tone set (row). Does any relation exist between the first and second halves (hexachords)? Then mirror (invert) the row a m6 higher. Finally, retrograde it a M6 lower.

I↑m6   (I⁸)

R↓M6   (R³)

2. Mirror (or invert) the intervals.   **3.** Transpose a m3 higher.

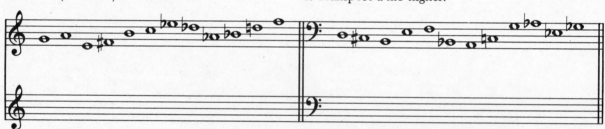

4. Transpose the retrograde a P4 higher.   **5.** Mirror (or invert) the retrograde.

6. Which of the above is not a twelve-tone row? _____

R. "The Moon Rises" is based upon the following set, in its prime zero form exclusively.

Trace the row throughout the music, using the numbering system indicated.

0   1   2   3   4   5   6   7   8   9   10   11

Krenek, "The Moon Rises," from *Twelve Short Piano Pieces,* Op. 83

S. Using the row found in "The Moon Rises," compose a two-voice composition, the upper voice of which is based on prime zero, while the lower makes use of retrograde zero. You might wish to compose this for instruments other than piano, such as violin and cello or two flutes.

T. The row shown below provides the basis for Berg's *Lyric Suite*. Complete the Babbitt Square, showing the various set forms and their transpositions. Number the prime and inversion forms in ascending order (chromatically) above the starting pitch. What is interesting about the original pitch set?

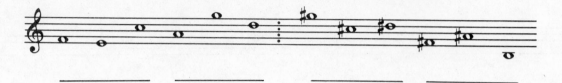

_____   _____   _____   _____

In the space provided, indicate prime forms for each of the trichords

comprising the row. What does this reveal? _____

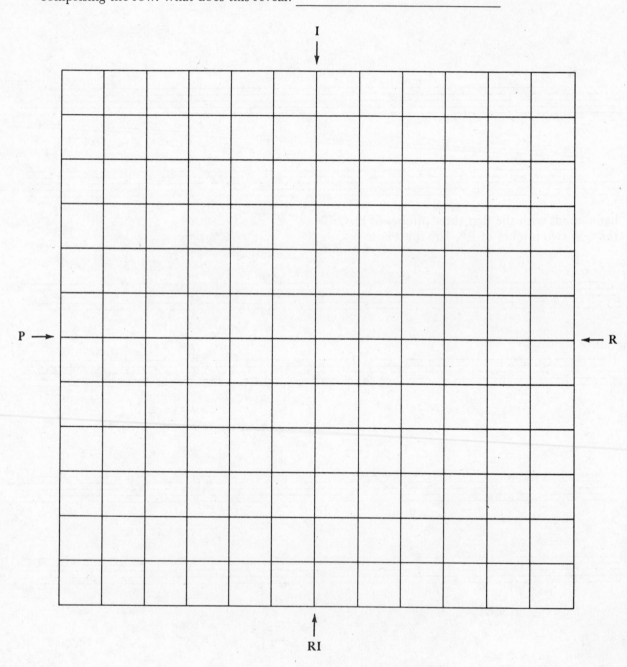

U. "Glass Figures," which follows, is based on the same row used in "The Moon Rises," but in its I⁰ and R⁰ forms. Write out these row forms on the staves provided:

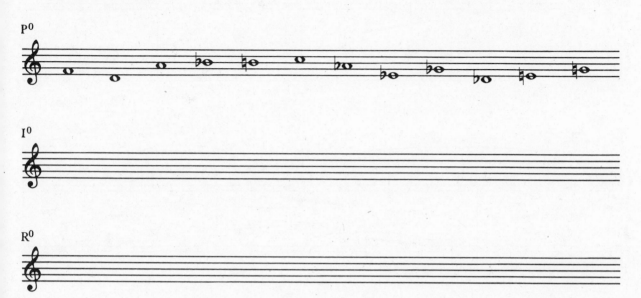

P⁰

I⁰

R⁰

In examining the music, you will note that the first measure of the right hand opens with the first three pitches of I⁰, while the left hand features the first two pitches of R⁰. The third note of this latter set, D♭, is accommodated by the right hand, since the third pitch of I⁰ is also a D♭. Following this, the roles of the set forms are reversed, with the left hand picking up I⁰ while the right hand continues with R⁰. Because of the frequency of this type of exchange where two or more row forms are involved, it is advisable to use different colored pencils to indicate different pitch collections in operation.

Krenek, "Glass Figures," from *Twelve Short Piano Pieces,* Op. 83

V. Examine the *Triad Study in B* and answer the following questions:

1. Although the piece is described as being "in B," what harmonic and melodic events in the opening five measures tend to obscure the tonal center? _____

_____

2. Describe the root relationship of the three triads found in mm. 3-4._____

_____

3. What key is hinted at in mm. 13-17? _____

4. In the space provided, show the root of each chord in mm. 19-24: _____

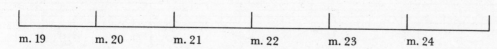

m. 19   m. 20   m. 21   m. 22   m. 23   m. 24

What do you find to be the predominant characteristic of the root movement in this passage?

5. The closing five measures seem to reveal a "tug-of-war" between the "official" key center and the key of _____ . Why? _____

_____

_____

Payne, *Triad Study in B*

W. Find scores and listen to recordings of works that illustrate the compositional principles mentioned in this chapter. Then try the following assignments:

1. Compose a short piece featuring aleatoric or indeterminate elements. Prepare a performance for class.

2. Analyze and write a summary of a piece that combines live and recorded music. Based upon your findings, compose a piece in this style.

3. Compose a piece featuring special effects for your instrument or voice. Perform the piece in class.

4. Select a three-note cell which will form the basis for a minimalist piece. Your composition should be based entirely upon permutations, transpositions, and rhythmic modifications of this cell. Experiment with various timbres and registers. Have the piece performed in class. Be sure that your performance directions are perfectly clear. (Hint: Your class performance will go much better if you arrange at least a brief rehearsal first!)